Pesticides

Current
CONTROVERSIES

Other Books in the Current Controversies Series

Assisted Suicide

Developing Nations

E-books

Family Violence

Gays in the Military

Global Warming

Human Trafficking

The Iranian Green Movement

Jobs in America

Medical Ethics

Modern-Day Piracy

Oil Spills

Pakistan

Politics and Religion

Pollution

Rap and Hip-Hop

Vaccines

Violence in the Media

Women in Politics

Pesticides

Debra A. Miller, Book Editor

GREENHAVEN PRESS
A part of Gale, Cengage Learning

GALE
CENGAGE Learning·

Farmington Hills, Mich • San Francisco • New York • Waterville, Maine
Meriden, Conn • Mason, Ohio • Chicago

Pesticides

APR 1 8 2014

GALE
CENGAGE Learning·

Elizabeth Des Chenes, *Director, Content Strategy*
Cynthia Sanner, *Publisher*
Douglas Dentino, *Manager, New Product*

© 2014 Greenhaven Press, a part of Gale, Cengage Learning

WCN: 01-100-101

Gale and Greenhaven Press are registered trademarks used herein under license.

For more information, contact:
Greenhaven Press
27500 Drake Rd.
Farmington Hills, MI 48331-3535
Or you can visit our Internet site at gale.cengage.com

For product information and technology assistance, contact us at

Gale Customer Support, 1-800-877-4253
For permission to use material from this text or product, submit all requests online at www.cengage.com/permissions

Further permissions questions can be emailed to permissionrequest@cengage.com

Articles in Greenhaven Press anthologies are often edited for length to meet page requirements. In addition, original titles of these works are changed to clearly present the main thesis and to explicitly indicate the author's opinion. Every effort is made to ensure that Greenhaven Press accurately reflects the original intent of the authors. Every effort has been made to trace the owners of copyrighted material.

Cover image copyright © Federico Rostagno/Shutterstock.com.

LIBRARY OF CONGRESS CATALOGING-IN-PUBLICATION DATA

Pesticides / Debra A. Miller, book editor.
    pages cm. -- (Current controversies)
    Summary: "Each anthology is composed of a wide spectrum of primary sources written by many of the foremost authorities in their respective fields. This unique approach provides students with a concise view of divergent opinions on each topic. Extensive book and periodical bibliographies and a list of organizations to contact are also included"-- Provided by publisher.
    Includes bibliographical references and index.
    ISBN 978-0-7377-6882-4 (hardback) -- ISBN 978-0-7377-6883-1 (paperback)
    1. Pesticides. 2. Pesticides--Health aspects. 3. Pesticides--Environmental aspects. 4. Pesticides--Government policy. I. Miller, Debra A.
    SB951.14.P47 2014
    363.738'498--dc23
                                                        2013033397

Printed in the United States of America
  1 2 3 4 5   18 17 16 15 14

Contents

Chapter 1: Do Pesticides Negatively Affect Human Health?

Yes: Pesticides Negatively Affect Human Health

A 2012 Stanford University study that downplayed the health risks of pesticides on conventional foods actually confirmed that organic foods have significantly lower levels of pesticides. The study also was defective in a number of ways, including the method used to assess risk levels and the fact that it ignored evidence that even low levels of pesticide exposure is especially dangerous for pregnant women and children.

David C. Holzman

A 2012 Stanford University study found little difference between organic and conventional foods in terms of pesticide health risks, but scientists in the environmental health field have criticized the study. Critics claim that Stanford used misleading risk metrics and ignored some studies that suggest that prenatal pesticide exposure can result in lower intelligence levels in children and higher disease rates.

No: Pesticides Do Not Negatively Affect Human Health

SafeFruitsandVeggies.com

According to a panel of experts assembled by the Alliance for Food and Farming, media stories about the dangers of pesticides in fruits and vegetables are causing some consumers to eat less of these healthy foods—a trend that may be contributing to record levels of obesity in the United States. Media reports emphasize the risks and ignore the well-documented benefits of eating fruits and vegetables grown under both conventional and organic conditions.

Michelle Brandt

Many consumers believe it is healthier to eat organic fruits and vegetables, and that it is worth paying extra for organic foods. However, a Stanford University study published in 2012 concluded that although organic foods have about a 30 percent lower risk of pesticide contamination than conventional foods, the pesticide levels of all foods fall within safety limits.

All pesticides, including natural pesticides used in organic agriculture, are toxic if consumed in high doses. But the level of pesticides in organic as well as conventionally grown foods is very low and there is no scientific evidence that they pose a significant threat to human health.

Chapter 2: How Are Pesticides Affecting the Environment?

Pesticide chemicals are toxic and when introduced into the environment can upset fragile ecosystems and cause serious problems. Examples of damage to the environment include shrinking honeybee populations, dramatic hormonal changes in frogs, and sudden bat deaths.

According to a recent report from the Organization for Economic Cooperation and Development (OECD), water pollution from agriculture is already causing serious environmental damage in developed countries and will only increase in the future with the economic rise of countries such as China and India.

Researchers from the Harvard School of Public Health have concluded that imidacloprid, a widely used pesticide, is the cause behind collapsing honeybee colonies in the United States. Finding and correcting the honeybee decline is extremely important because honeybees are needed to pollinate one-third of US crops.

DDT has historically been used to combat malaria in the developing world, but the parasites that cause malaria have increasingly become resistant to the pesticide. Many countries, such as Mexico, have abandoned DDT in favor of greener methods of fighting malaria, such as draining bodies of water where mosquitoes hatch their eggs.

Chapter 3: Are Pesticides Needed in Agriculture for World Food Production?

Large pesticide manufacturers try to market the idea that pesticides are essential to food production, but crop losses have actually increased as more and more pesticides are used. Pesticides are dangerous even in small amounts and the government regulatory system is not doing a good job of protecting people from these chemicals.

Chapter 4: What Is the Future for Pesticides?

Foreword

By definition, controversies are "discussions of questions in which opposing opinions clash" (*Webster's Twentieth Century Dictionary Unabridged*). Few would deny that controversies are a pervasive part of the human condition and exist on virtually every level of human enterprise. Controversies transpire between individuals and among groups, within nations and between nations. Controversies supply the grist necessary for progress by providing challenges and challengers to the status quo. They also create atmospheres where strife and warfare can flourish. A world without controversies would be a peaceful world; but it also would be, by and large, static and prosaic.

The Series' Purpose

The purpose of the Current Controversies series is to explore many of the social, political, and economic controversies dominating the national and international scenes today. Titles selected for inclusion in the series are highly focused and specific. For example, from the larger category of criminal justice, Current Controversies deals with specific topics such as police brutality, gun control, white collar crime, and others. The debates in Current Controversies also are presented in a useful, timeless fashion. Articles and book excerpts included in each title are selected if they contribute valuable, long-range ideas to the overall debate. And wherever possible, current information is enhanced with historical documents and other relevant materials. Thus, while individual titles are current in focus, every effort is made to ensure that they will not become quickly outdated. Books in the Current Controversies series will remain important resources for librarians, teachers, and students for many years.

In addition to keeping the titles focused and specific, great care is taken in the editorial format of each book in the series. Book introductions and chapter prefaces are offered to provide background material for readers. Chapters are organized around several key questions that are answered with diverse opinions representing all points on the political spectrum. Materials in each chapter include opinions in which authors clearly disagree as well as alternative opinions in which authors may agree on a broader issue but disagree on the possible solutions. In this way, the content of each volume in Current Controversies mirrors the mosaic of opinions encountered in society. Readers will quickly realize that there are many viable answers to these complex issues. By questioning each author's conclusions, students and casual readers can begin to develop the critical thinking skills so important to evaluating opinionated material.

Current Controversies is also ideal for controlled research. Each anthology in the series is composed of primary sources taken from a wide gamut of informational categories including periodicals, newspapers, books, US and foreign government documents, and the publications of private and public organizations. Readers will find factual support for reports, debates, and research papers covering all areas of important issues. In addition, an annotated table of contents, an index, a book and periodical bibliography, and a list of organizations to contact are included in each book to expedite further research.

Perhaps more than ever before in history, people are confronted with diverse and contradictory information. During the Persian Gulf War, for example, the public was not only treated to minute-to-minute coverage of the war, it was also inundated with critiques of the coverage and countless analyses of the factors motivating US involvement. Being able to sort through the plethora of opinions accompanying today's major issues, and to draw one's own conclusions, can be a complicated and frustrating struggle. It is the editors' hope that Current Controversies will help readers with this struggle.

Introduction

"There are indications that people used natural pesticides thousands of years ago, but the widespread use of synthetic chemical pesticides is a relatively recent phenomenon that developed during and after World War II."

Pesticides are used to kill pests—broadly defined as anything that humans decide are a problem to humans. Under the heading of pesticides are a variety of products, including, for example, insecticides that target insects, herbicides to eradicate weeds, rodenticides that kill rodents, and fungicides that attack fungi, among many others. The United States is the world's biggest user of pesticides. About 75 percent of pesticides are used in US agriculture, but most American households also use pesticides to kill weeds or insects in and around the home. There are indications that people used natural pesticides thousands of years ago, but the widespread use of synthetic chemical pesticides is a relatively recent phenomenon that developed during and after World War II.

The first type of pesticide used by humans appears to have been sulfur—a naturally occurring substance that was used by the ancient Sumarians as early as 2500 BC to control insects and mites. There is also evidence that the Chinese employed sulfur around 1000 BC to control bacteria and mold. The Chinese also discovered that mercury and arsenic, natural poisons, could be used to kill body lice. Ancient Greeks and Romans, meanwhile, used smoke from the burning of straw, dung, or other materials to dispel insects, blight, or mildew from plants. And Persians used salt to control weeds and pyrethrum powder, a substance obtained from the dried flowers of a plant called Chrysanthemum cinerariaefolium, to protect grain harvests.

As agriculture developed, these and other types of natural or nonsynthetic pesticides continued to be used over many centuries to help protect crops against weeds, diseases, insects, rodents, and other pests. Other natural pesticides that developed in later years include nicotine, an extract from the leaves of tobacco plants used as an insecticide, and rotenone, an insecticide obtained from the roots of a plant found in Southeast Asia, Derris elliptica. Rotenone is still used today by organic farmers. Many of these natural pesticides, however, are difficult to produce in large quantities, so historically their use has been limited.

The modern pesticide industry really did not begin until after World War II, when a host of new, very potent synthetic pesticides were introduced and marketed to the public. Many of the new synthetic pesticides—meaning products created by chemistry—were originally developed secretly during the war to be used as chemical warfare agents. When the war ended, some of these chemical compounds were promoted as insecticides for agriculture. In 1937, for example, German chemists developed a class of synthetic pesticides called organophosphates that are still being used today.

Another type of synthetic pesticide developed during the war and during the postwar period was a class of pesticides known as dioxins. One of these dioxin pesticides, DDT (dichloro-diphenyl-trichloroethane), soon became very popular and was used extensively in the United States, largely because it was easy to apply and could be used to kill a wide variety of insects. In fact, Dr. Paul Müller won the 1948 Nobel Prize in Physiology or Medicine for the discovery of the insecticidal properties of DDT. However, many insects quickly developed resistance to DDT. In addition, scientists found that DDT continued to be highly toxic in the environment even after it was diluted by rainwater. In 1962, biologist and conservationist Rachel Carson published a book, *Silent Spring*, that described in detail how DDT was causing environmental pollution, killing birds and fish, accumulating in the fatty tissues of animals and humans, and resulting in serious human health problems like cancer and genetic damage. Carson warned that pesticides could ultimately destroy the Earth's fragile ecosystems. The book created a public uproar and led to the birth of the environmental movement in the United States. In addition, *Silent Spring* is often credited with prompting President Richard Nixon, in 1970, to form a new federal antipollution agency—the US Environmental Protection Agency (EPA). In 1972, after studies clearly showed DDT to be a human carcinogen, the EPA banned the use of this pesticide in the United States, although it continues to be used in many developing countries even today.

Despite the successful banning of DDT, pesticide use has only grown since the 1960s. Each year for the next twenty years the amount of pesticides applied on American farms increased dramatically. In addition, the chemical and pesticide industries developed many new types of pesticides that tend to be both more soluble in water and more toxic—qualities that many antipesticide advocates claim is leading to even greater environmental damage and a continuing threat to human health. Today, according to a report issued by the EPA in 2011, close to a billion pounds of toxic chemicals are applied to American lands, more than 75 percent of it on farms where food crops are grown.

Large-scale farmers and agribusiness corporations claim that these chemical pesticides have been properly tested to ensure that they are safe and that they are essential to producing high-quality food. Environmentalists, however, maintain that pesticides are wrecking the natural environment—including soils, ground water, wild birds, and animals—as well as contributing to a host of human health problems such as allergies, hormonal imbalances, nerve damage, and cancer. The authors of the viewpoints included in *Current Controversies: Pesticides* examine some of the issues important in the debate about pesticides, including whether they are negatively affecting human health, how they are interacting with the environment, whether they are needed to feed the world, and what might happen in the future.

CHAPTER 1

Do Pesticides Negatively Affect Human Health?

Chapter Preface

One of the biggest controversies surrounding the use of synthetic pesticides is what amount of pesticides are still present on the vegetables and fruit once they reach the market and whether these pesticides can harm human health. To help consumers navigate supermarket produce aisles and choose the least toxic fruits and vegetables, the Environmental Working Group (EWG)—a nonprofit health and environmental advocacy organization—publishes an annual *Shopper's Guide to Pesticides in Produce*. This guide provides information about the pesticide content of dozens of fruits and vegetables grown conventionally—that is, using chemical pesticides—based on pesticide residue testing data from the US Department of Agriculture (USDA) and the US Food and Drug Administration (FDA). EWG advises consumers to reduce their pesticide exposure as much as possible by avoiding produce ranked highest in pesticide residue and buying foods that have the lowest pesticide loads. At the same time, however, EWG urges people to eat lots of fruits and vegetables and says that eating conventionally grown fruits and vegetables with pesticides is healthier than not eating fresh produce at all.

EWG's list is divided into two parts. One part, called the "Dirty Dozen," lists the produce that contains the highest amount of pesticides. EWG recommends that consumers always buy these fruits and vegetables in their organic form—that is, grown on organic instead of conventional farms. In 2012, however, EWG expanded the Dirty Dozen list to include three vegetables—green beans, kale, and collard greens—that are often contaminated with organophosphate insecticides—a type of pesticide that has been found to be highly toxic to human nervous systems. Organophosphates are not used as much as they once were in US agriculture, EWG has explained, but they are not officially banned and sometimes are still present on produce. In addition, EWG notes that almost all commodity crop sweet corn, which is grown mostly for animal feed and biofuels but which also is sometimes sold as human food, is grown using genetically modified (GMO) seeds. This corn does not contain a label identifying it as a GMO product, so EWG advises consumers concerned about GMO foods to buy organic sweet corn. The Dirty Dozen list for 2013 contains the following fruits and vegetables:

1. Apples
2. Celery
3. Sweet bell peppers
4. Peaches
5. Strawberries
6. Imported nectarines
7. Grapes
8. Spinach
9. Lettuce
10. Cucumbers
11. Domestic blueberries
12. Potatoes
13. Green Beans
14. Kale
15. Greens (e.g., collard greens)

The second part of EWG's *Shopper's Guide* is the "Clean Fifteen"—fifteen types of produce found to have the least amount of pesticides. EWG recommends that consumers who cannot afford to buy all organic produce buy organic Dirty Dozen produce and then buy fruits and vegetables on the

Clean Fifteen list in their conventional form. The 2012 Clean Fifteen list includes the following items:

1. Onions

2. Sweet corn

3. Pineapples

4. Avocado

5. Cabbage

6. Sweet peas

7. Asparagus

8. Mangoes

9. Eggplant

10. Kiwi

11. Domestic cantaloupe

12. Sweet potatoes

13. Grapefruit

14. Watermelon

15. Mushrooms

Other highlights in EWG's 2012 report include the fact that imported nectarines contained more pesticides than any other food crop. EWG explains that every sample of imported nectarines contained pesticides, as did most apples (98 percent) and plums (96 percent). Meanwhile, grapes were found to have more types of pesticides than any other produce—64 different pesticides—while grapes, domestic blueberries, and strawberries had the most pesticides per sample. Similarly, most celery (96 percent) and potatoes (91 percent) were contaminated with pesticides, while bell peppers, cucumbers, and lettuce all tested positive for dozens of different types of pesticides.

EWG also highlighted baby foods in its 2012 report. The report notes that the USDA in 2012 tested about 190 samples of green bean, pear, and sweet potato baby foods and found significant levels of pesticides on both green bean and pear foods. The green bean baby food tested positive for five pesticides, including organophosphate pesticides that can damage the brain and nervous system. EWG concluded that children eating four ounces of green bean baby food daily could be at serious risk. Similarly, most of the pear samples tested by the USDA were found to have residue from between one and five pesticides, some containing iprodione, a pesticide that the EPA has categorized as a probable human carcinogen. Only sweet potato baby food was found to have virtually no detectable pesticides.

Advocates representing the fruit and vegetable industry have criticized the EWG *Shopper's Guide* for scaring consumers away from conventionally grown produce and helping the organic produce industry. In 2012, for example, the Alliance for Food and Farming published a report called "Scared Fat," which argued that consumers are less likely to buy and eat fruits and vegetables because of media messages about their pesticide content, and are eating less healthy foods as a result. The authors of the viewpoints included in this chapter debate this critical question of whether pesticides are negatively affecting human health.

Pesticides Have Been Associated with Many Different Health Dangers

Toxics Action Center

The Toxics Action Center is a New England-based advocacy organization dedicated to fighting pollution problems and protecting the health of people and the environment.

Pesticides are the only toxic substances released intentionally into our environment to kill living things. This includes substances that kill weeds (herbicides), insects (insecticides), fungus (fungicides), rodents (rodenticides), and others.

The use of toxic pesticides to manage pest problems has become a common practice around the world. Pesticides are used almost everywhere—not only in agricultural fields, but also in homes, parks, schools, buildings, forests, and roads. It is difficult to find somewhere where pesticides aren't used—from the can of bug spray under the kitchen sink to the airplane crop dusting acres of farmland, our world is filled with pesticides. In addition, pesticides can be found in the air we breathe, the food we eat, and the water we drink.

When Rachel Carson wrote *Silent Spring* in 1962, she raised public awareness about the effects of pesticide use on our health and our environment. However, almost forty years after Carson drew attention to the health and environmental impacts of DDT [dichlorodiphenyltrichloroethane, an insecticide], use of equally hazardous pesticides has only increased. And all the time there is more evidence surfacing that human exposure to pesticides is linked to health problems. For example, in May 2010, scientists from the University of Montreal and Harvard University released a study that found that exposure to pesticide residues on vegetables and fruit may double a child's risk of attention deficit hyperactivity disorder (ADHD), a condition that can cause inattention, hyperactivity, and impulsivity in children.

Pesticides are used in our schools, parks, and public lands. Pesticides are sprayed on agricultural fields and wood lots. Pesticides can be found in our air, our food, our soil, our water and even in our breast milk.

Pesticides and Human Health

Pesticides have been linked to a wide range of human health hazards, ranging from short-term impacts such as headaches and nausea to chronic impacts like cancer, reproductive harm, and endocrine disruption.

Pesticides can cause many types of cancer in humans. Some of the most prevalent forms include leukemia, nonHodgkins lymphoma, brain, bone, breast, ovarian, prostate, testicular and liver cancers.

Acute dangers—such as nerve, skin, and eye irritation and damage, headaches, dizziness, nausea, fatigue, and systemic poisoning—can sometimes be dramatic, and even occasionally fatal.

Chronic health effects may occur years after even minimal exposure to pesticides in the environment, or result from the pesticide residues which we ingest through our food and water. A July 2007 study conducted by researchers at the Public Health Institute, the California Department of Health Services, and the UC [University of California] Berkeley School of Public Health found a sixfold increase in risk factor for autism spectrum disorders (ASD) for children of women who were exposed to organochlorine pesticides.

Pesticides can cause many types of cancer in humans. Some of the most prevalent forms include leukemia, non-Hodgkins lymphoma, brain, bone, breast, ovarian, prostate, testicular and liver cancers. In February 2009, the Agency for Toxic Substances and Disease Registry published a study that found that children who live in homes where their parents use pesticides are twice as likely to develop brain cancer versus those that live in residences in which no pesticides are used.

Studies by the National Cancer Institute found that American farmers, who in most respects are healthier than the population at large, had startling incidences of leukemia, Hodgkins disease, non-Hodgkins lymphoma, and many other forms of cancer.

There is also mounting evidence that exposure to pesticides disrupts the endocrine system, wreaking havoc with the complex regulation of hormones, the reproductive system, and embryonic development. Endocrine disruption can produce infertility and a variety of birth defects and developmental defects in offspring, including hormonal imbalance and incomplete sexual development, impaired brain development, behavioral disorders, and many others. Examples of known endocrine disrupting chemicals which are present in large quantities in our environment include DDT (which still persists in abundance more than 20 years after being banned in the U.S.), lindane, atrazine, carbaryl, parathion, and many others.

Children are particularly susceptible to the hazards associated with pesticide use.

Multiple Chemical Sensitivity (MCS) is a medical condition characterized by the body's inability to tolerate relatively low exposure to chemicals. This condition, also referred to as Environmental Illness, is triggered by exposure to certain chemicals and/or environmental pollutants. Exposure to pesticides is a common way for individuals to develop MCS, and once the condition is present, pesticides are often a potent trigger for symptoms of the condition. The variety of these symptoms can be dizzying, including everything from cardio-vascular problems to depression to muscle and joint pains. Over time, individuals suffering from MCS will begin to react adversely to substances that formerly did not affect them.

For individuals suffering from MCS, the only way to re-lieve their symptoms is to avoid those substances that trigger adverse reactions. For some individuals, this can mean almost complete isolation from the outside world.

Pesticides and Children

Children are particularly susceptible to the hazards associated with pesticide use. There is now considerable scientific evi-dence that the human brain is not fully formed until the age of 12, and childhood exposure to some of the most common pesticides on the market may greatly impact the development of the central nervous system. Children have more skin sur-face for their size than adults, absorb proportionally greater amounts of many substances through their lungs and intesti-nal tracts, and take in more air, food and water per pound than adults. Children have not developed their immune sys-tems, nervous systems, or detoxifying mechanisms completely, leaving them less capable of fighting the introduction of toxic pesticides into their systems.

Many of the activities that children engage in—playing in the grass, putting objects into their mouth and even playing on carpet—increase their exposure to toxic pesticides. The combination of likely increased exposure to pesticides and lack of bodily development to combat the toxic effects of pes-ticides means that children are suffering disproportionately from their impacts.

Pesticides and the Environment

Since the publication of Rachel Carson's landmark 1962 book *Silent Spring*, the impacts of pesticides on the environment have been well known. Pesticides are toxic to living organisms. Some can accumulate in water systems, pollute the air, and in some cases have other dramatic environmental effects. Scientists are discovering new threats to the environment that are equally disturbing.

According to the US EPA, more than 70 active ingredients known to cause cancer in animal tests are allowed for use.

Pesticide use can damage agricultural land by harming beneficial insect species, soil microorganisms, and worms which naturally limit pest populations and maintain soil health; weakening plant root systems and immune systems; and reducing concentrations of essential plant nutrients in the soil such nitrogen and phosphorous.

The Myth of Safety: A Failed Regulatory System

Despite what government agencies and corporations tell you, pesticide products currently on the market are not safe, even when they are used legally. There are many flaws in the way that pesticides are registered and in our political process that allows corporations to influence pesticide policy to allow the continued use of their poisonous products.

Even if we know that a pesticide causes severe health and environmental impacts, including cancer and genetic damage, it may still be allowed for use. The EPA [US Environmental Protection Agency] may determine that a cancer-causing chemical may be used despite its public health hazard if its "economic, social or environmental" benefits are deemed greater than its risk. According to the U.S. EPA, more than 70 active ingredients known to cause cancer in animal tests are allowed for use.

Although industry tests for a wide range of environmental and health impacts, the vast majority of pesticides currently on the market have not been fully tested.

Pesticides often contain inert ingredients in addition to the active ingredients that are designed to kill the target pest. Unfortunately, the public is not provided information about what inert ingredients are included in pesticides in most cases.

At least 382 of the chemicals that the U.S. EPA lists as inert ingredients were once or are currently also registered as pesticide active ingredients. This means that the public is kept in the dark about the contents of pesticide products that may be hazardous. Among the ingredients that are listed as both inert and active ingredients are chloropicrin, which has been linked to asthma and pulmonary edema, and chlorothanonil, a probable human carcinogen.

The Solution to Pesticides

We need to make our food, our air, our water, and our soil free from toxic chemicals.

The real solution to our pest and weed problems lies in non-toxic and cultural methods of agriculture, not in pulling the pesticide trigger. Organically grown foods and sustainable methods of pest control are key to our families' health and the health of the environment.

Better testing. State and federal agencies should require stricter independent testing, including testing of synergistic effects of pesticides. Pesticides known or suspected of causing human health problems should be phased out.

Protect our children. Because our children are the most vulnerable population to pesticides, pesticide use should be prohibited in places where our children live and play, including schools, parks, and playgrounds. Require strict non-toxic pest management programs for such places.

Pesticide Use Reduction. Provide technical assistance to farmers, local governments, businesses, and homeowners on non-toxic alternatives to pesticide use. This includes alternatives to nuisance spraying for mosquitoes and controlling West Nile virus and other pest problems.

Prohibit pollution of our water and poisoning of our communities. Ensure that aerial pesticide use does not pollute our waterways through strict rules governing spraying and buffer zones that prevent the harmful effects of drift. Prohibit the use of pesticides for purely aesthetic reasons. Prevent pesticide applications to water bodies, instead using non-chemical methods of managing aquatic invasive weeds.

Right to know. Provide free and universal notification to residents about pesticide use, including who is using chemicals, where, when, how, what pesticides are being used, and why.

Protect workers. Provide protection to workers and farmers to prevent acute and chronic pesticide poisoning.

Even Low Levels of Pesticides Can Have Serious Health Effects on Children

Elizabeth Sharpe

Elizabeth Sharpe is the communication director at the University of Washington's Department of Environmental and Occupational Health Sciences.

Increasing evidence shows urban and rural children are regularly exposed to low levels of pesticides that can have serious long-term health effects, according to a report issued by the American Academy of Pediatrics [AAP].

The technical report and an accompanying policy statement on pesticide exposure in children appear in the December 2012 issue of *Pediatrics*.

Dr. Catherine Karr, an environmental health pediatrician in the UW [University of Washington] School of Public Health and the School of Medicine, co-authored both papers, which recommend public and professional approaches to the issue of childhood pesticide exposure.

Pediatricians don't get this information or training in their routine medical education and are likely not aware of the wealth of studies that have been published up to now on the subject, said Karr, who served on the American Academy of Pediatrics' Council on Environmental Health from 2005–2011. She believes doctors can play a significant role in protecting children's health by recognizing, treating, and preventing exposure to pesticides.

The Pesticide Threat to Children

The ubiquitous chemicals are as varied as their uses. For example, lawns are treated with weed killer, sprays or foggers kill fleas indoors, and pesticides control coddling moths that can destroy large-scale apple production.

Children are more vulnerable to the harmful effects of pesticides than are adults because of their smaller size and faster metabolism.

Karr observed that the product label, "while providing some information on acute toxicity, doesn't inform consumers or workers about chronic toxicity, such as whether the product contains a carcinogen or whether it is linked to reproductive or developmental toxicity."

Epidemiological studies associate both acute and chronic pesticide exposures in children with pediatric cancer and neurodevelopmental disorders. Pesticide exposure has even been implicated with attention deficit hyperactivity disorder and low-birth weight.

Children are more vulnerable to the harmful effects of pesticides than are adults because of their smaller size and faster metabolism. Youngsters can be exposed by breathing the chemicals in the air, getting them on their skin, or unintentionally ingesting the pesticides. Kids crawl or play on surfaces that may have chemical residues, and they often put their fingers and other objects in their month.

The dietary contribution from food residues provides cumulative, chronic exposure.

"For most kids in the United States, it's probably the major component," said Karr. She pointed to a study on children's diet by alumnus Chensheng Lu, who received a Ph.D. in 1996 from the UW in industrial hygiene and safety. He is now on faculty at Harvard University. His study was conducted with researchers in the Pacific Northwest Agricultural Safety and Health Center at the UW.

For five days, the researchers substituted most of children's conventional diets with organic food items. They measured the metabolites for organophosphorus pesticides in the children's urine and compared the levels before and after changes in diet. They found the metabolites disappeared after the organic diet was introduced and remained undetectable until the conventional diet was reintroduced.

These results shouldn't be interpreted to mean non-organic food is bad. Karr notes a recent American Academy of Pediatrics review on organic foods found no evidence that the nutritional content varies, and the health benefits of fresh fruits and vegetables in children's diet are clear.

"Given the often increased expense, some families might choose to be selective in choosing organic foods," she said. "The levels of pesticide residues tend to be lower in some conventionally grown fruits and vegetables and consumer guides are readily available on these topics."

She also recommends thoroughly washing produce. Karr published tips for parents on reducing their child's exposure to pesticides in food and from other common sources.

Educating Doctors

Of the numerous recommendations to doctors and policymakers in the published statement, one resonates very clearly for Karr

"I think we could make a big difference if all healthcare providers who take care of children felt they had a basic knowledge base on pesticides that enabled them to include pesticide safety counseling in routine health visits and to think about pesticide exposure in relevant sick visits," said Karr, who also put together a guide for pediatricians on how to talk with parents about pesticides. It's available on AAP's website.

The technical report details the major classes of pesticides, their adverse health effects, and evaluation and treatment. Symptoms of pesticide exposure might not be easily recognized, explained Karr. In one case, a child might have a rash or a headache. In another case, a child might be vomiting or have diarrhea.

"Having pesticide exposure in your mind as a possibility," she noted, "requires an index of suspicion which you develop only when you know a little bit about pesticides and what you can do."

Healthcare providers might also be interested in a local resource. Karr directs the Northwest Pediatric Environmental Health Specialty Unit based at the UW. The unit provides expertise and training for health professionals, trainees, and the public on environmentally related health effects in children, including pesticide exposure. In collaboration with the UW Center for Child Environmental Health Risks Research led by Elaine M. Faustman, professor of environmental health, and with corresponding research center partners in California, the Northwest Pediatric Environmental Health Specialty Unit is creating an educational module on pesticides.

A Stanford University Study Underestimates the Health Risks of Pesticides in Conventionally Grown Foods

Tom Philpott

Tom Philpott is the food and agriculture blogger for Mother Jones, *a progressive news magazine. He also has written for the online environmental site* Grist *and various other magazines and newspapers.*

Is organic food little more than a trumped-up marketing scheme, another way for affluent consumers to waste money? A just-released paper by Stanford University researchers—and the reaction to it by the media—suggests as much.

"Stanford Scientists Cast Doubt on Advantages of Organic Meat and Produce," declared a *New York Times* headline. "Organic food hardly healthier, study suggests," announced *CBS News*. "Is organic healthier? Study says not so much, but it's key reason consumers buy," the *Washington Post* grumbled.

In reality, though, the study in some places makes a strong case for organic—though you'd barely know it from the language the authors use. And in places where it finds organic wanting, key information gets left out. To assess the state of science on organic food and its health benefits, the authors performed what's known among academics as a "meta-analysis"—they gathered all the research papers they could find on the topic dating back decades, eliminated ones that didn't meet their criteria for scientific rigor, and summarized the results.

In another post I'll get to the question of nutritional benefits—the idea, expressed by the Stanford authors, that organic and conventional foods are roughly equivalent in terms of vitamins and other nutrients. What I want to discuss now is the problem of pesticide exposure, and why I think the Stanford researchers are underestimating the risks.

A Case for Organic Produce

In short, the authors' findings confirm what the Environmental Working Group, crunching USDA [US Department of Agriculture] data, has been telling us for years: that organic fruits and vegetables harbor significantly fewer pesticide residues than their chemically grown peers. Summing up the evidence of the studies they looked at, the Stanford researchers find what they call a 30 percent "risk difference" between organic and conventional food—which to the mind not trained in statistics, sounds like organic foods carry 30 percent less risk of exposing you to pesticides. And they immediately undercut that finding by noting that the pesticide traces found in both organic and conventional food tend to be at levels lower than the Environmental Protection Agency's maximum allowed limits. Takeaway: Conventional produce carries trivially small levels of pesticides, and you might as well save your money and forget organic.

High-risk pesticides rarely appear as residues in organic food, and when they do, the levels are usually much lower than those found in conventional food.

What's wrong with this comforting picture?

1. Conventional produce is much worse than organic on the pesticide-exposure question than the 30 percent number suggests. That's what Chuck Benbrook, research professor at Washington State University's Center for Sustaining Agriculture and Natural Resources, shows in a detailed critique of the study.

To get the 30 percent number, the authors used an odd statistical construct they call "risk difference." By their method, if 5 percent of organic vegetables contain at least one pesticide trace and 35 percent of conventional vegetables contain at least one trace, then the "risk difference" is 30 percent (35 minus 5). But that's a silly way of thinking about it, because there's a much greater difference between those numbers than "30 percent" suggests. Crunching the authors' own raw data, Benbrook finds "an overall 81% lower risk or incidence of one or more pesticide residues in the organic samples compared to the conventional samples."

But even that doesn't get to the full extent of the study's underestimation, since:

2. To arrive at their "risk difference" metric, the authors didn't distinguish between a single pesticide trace and multiple traces; or between light traces and heavier traces. For their purposes, an organic apple carrying a tiny residue of a relatively innocuous pesticide is equivalent to a conventional apple containing a cocktail of several relatively toxic pesticides. Here's Benbrook on why that's silly: a) most residues in organic food occur at much lower levels than in conventional food, b) residues are not as likely in organic foods, c) multiple residues in a single sample are rare in organic food but common in conventional produce, and d) high-risk pesticides rarely appear as residues in organic food, and when they do, the levels are usually much lower than those found in conventional food (especially the levels in imported produce).

Now, the authors might reply that all of this is trivial, because the traces that researchers find on produce, whether conventional or organic, almost always come in at levels below the EPA's safety threshold. But:

3. This ignores a growing body of research that pregnant women's fetuses can be harmed at low exposures of organophosphate pesticides, as can young children.

And what's more:

4. *The authors—like the EPA [US Environmental Protection Agency] itself—ignore the "cocktail effect" of exposure to several pesticides, say, from a single apple.* As Environmental Working Group's analysis of USDA data shows, conventional produce like apples, blueberries, and bell peppers often carry traces of many pesticides. The EPA regulates pesticide traces only on an individual basis, disregarding possible synergistic effects. The European Commission is starting to take them more seriously. Here's a report commissioned by the European Commission in 2009:

There is a consensus in the field of mixture toxicology that the customary chemical-by-chemical approach to risk assessment might be too simplistic. It is in danger of underestimating the risk of chemicals to human health and to the environment.

Which brings us to the fifth point:

5. *We probably know more about how exposure to low levels of multiple pesticides affect amphibians than we do about how they affect people—and what our amphibious friends are telling us isn't pretty.*

In short, the Stanford study seriously underplays the benefit of going organic to avoid pesticide traces, especially for vulnerable populations like pregnant women and kids. In a future post, I'll show why it does the same for exposure to antibiotic-resistant pathogens in meat, and doesn't give organic its due with regard to nutritional benefits.

Organic Food Conclusions Don't Tell the Whole Story

David C. Holzman

David C. Holzman is a writer whose work on science, medicine, energy, and cars has appeared in Smithsonian, The Atlantic Monthly, *and the* Journal of the National Cancer Institute.

A widely reported Stanford University study[1] concluding there is little difference in the healthfulness and safety of conventional and organic foods has been criticized by experts in the environmental health sciences for overlooking the growing body of evidence on the adverse effects of pesticides. Critics take to task the authors' omission of relevant studies and overinterpretation of the data.

The meta-analysis of 237 studies, published in the September 2012 *Annals of Internal Medicine*, largely focused on nutrient content and viral/bacterial/fungal contamination of organic versus conventionally grown foods. Nine studies reporting pesticide residues, including three of residues exceeding federal limits, were included in summary analyses.

The authors concluded that the studies reviewed do not support what they call the "widespread perception" that organic foods overall are nutritionally superior to conventional ones, although eating an organic diet may reduce exposures to pesticides and antibiotic-resistant bacteria.[1] A Stanford press release quoted senior author Dena Bravata as saying, "There isn't much difference between organic and conventional foods, if you're an adult and making a decision based solely on your health."[2] (According to the Stanford Medical Center press office, Bravata is no longer doing interviews about the study.)

David C. Holzman, "Organic Food Conclusions Don't Tell the Whole Story," *Environmental Health Perspectives*, vol. 120, no. 12, December 3, 2012. Reproduced by permission.

In one key finding, the team reported a "risk difference" of 30% between conventional and organic produce, meaning organic produce had a 30% lower risk of pesticide contamination than conventional produce. That number was based on the difference between the percentages of conventional and organic food samples across studies with any detectible pesticide residues (38% and 7%, respectively).

The Stanford researchers . . . missed opportunities to examine the relationship of pesticides and health outcomes demonstrated in a growing number of cohort studies.

But the concept of risk difference is potentially misleading in this context, as the metric does not refer to health risk, according to Charles Benbrook, research professor and program leader for Measure to Manage (M2M): Farm and Food Diagnostics for Sustainability and Health at Washington State University. Furthermore, says Benbrook, "Pesticide dietary risk is a function of many factors, including the number of residues, their levels, and pesticide toxicity," not just whether contamination was present.

In a letter accepted for publication in the *Annals of Internal Medicine*,[3] Benbrook pointed to the Stanford team's lack of consideration of extensive government data on the number, frequency, potential combinations, and associated health risks of pesticide residues in U.S. food. Using data from the U.S. Department of Agriculture's Pesticide Data Program,[4] Benbrook calculated a 94% reduction in health risk attributable to eating organic forms of six pesticide-intensive fruits.[3]

The Stanford researchers also missed opportunities to examine the relationship of pesticides and health outcomes demonstrated in a growing number of cohort studies, says Brenda Eskenazi, a professor in the School of Public Health at the University of California, Berkeley. Eskenazi conducted one such study,[5] one of a trio published in April 2011 that examined the relationship between cognitive development and prenatal pesticide exposures in two multiethnic inner-city populations[6,7] and one farmworker community in California.[5] One of the studies[7] found deficits of seven IQ points in 7-year-old children in the highest quintile of pesticide exposure, compared with children in the lowest quintile, as measured by maternal urinary pesticide metabolite levels during pregnancy. Results were comparable in the other two studies.

In concluding that the evidence "does not suggest marked health benefits from consuming organic versus conventional foods,"[1] many commenters, including Eskenazi and Benbrook, felt the Stanford team ignored risks to broader public health like those outlined in an April 2012 review by David C. Bellinger, a professor of neurology at Harvard Medical School. In his review Bellinger argued that subtle impacts of organophosphate pesticides on neurodevelopment can add up to substantial population-level impacts. He wrote, "It is frequently noted that a modest downward shift in mean IQ scores will be accompanied by a substantial increase in the percentage of individuals with extremely low scores."[8]

Conventional toxicology testing is now being shown to miss responses that occur at doses that are orders of magnitude lower than previously established no-observed-adverse-effects levels,[9] with potential implications for our understanding of pesticide safety. And others are finding in animal studies that pesticide exposures *in utero* can induce epigenetic changes that alter stress responses and disease rates in future generations.

In one study, exposure of rats to vinclozolin, a common agricultural fungicide, was associated with altered stress responses in the F3 generation (the original animals' great grandchildren), compared with F3 progeny of unexposed animals.[10] These responses were seen at high doses unlikely to be encountered as food residues but potentially applicable to agricultural workers. Exposures to the pesticides methoxychlor,

DEET, permethrin, and vinclozolin, as well as dioxin, also "predispose animals to develop a variety of adult-onset diseases earlier than normal," says Michael Skinner, a professor in the Washington State University School of Biological Sciences who coauthored this study. He says these effects are "still detectable in animals over four subsequent generations, without diminution."

In October 2012 the American Academy of Pediatrics weighed in, for the first time ever, on the question of whether children benefit from an organic diet.[11] In a report published in *Pediatrics*, the academy recognized that an organic diet definitely reduces exposure to pesticides and may reduce diseases associated with antibiotic resistance but has not been proven to offer a clinically relevant nutritional advantage over a conventional diet. The academy emphasized the importance of providing children a diet rich in fruits, vegetables, whole grains, and low-fat or fat-free dairy products, regardless of whether the foods are conventional or organic, and provided resources for parents seeking guidance on which foods tend to have the heaviest pesticide residues.

References

1. Smith-Spangler C, et al. Are organic foods safer or healthier than conventional alternatives? A systematic review. Ann Intern Med 157(5):348–366 (2012); http://www.ncbi.nlm.nih.gov/pubmed/22944875.

2. Brandt M. Little evidence of health benefits from organic foods, Stanford study finds. Inside Stanford Medicine (3 Sep 2012). Stanford, CA:School of Medicine, Stanford University. Available: http://med.stanford.edu/ism/2012/september/organic.html [accessed 14 Nov 2012].

3. Benbrook C. Initial Reflections on the Annals of Internal Medicine Paper "Are Organic Foods Safer and Healthier

than Conventional Alternatives? A Systematic Review." Available: http://caff.org/wp-content/uploads/2010/07/Annals_Response_Final.pdf [accessed 14 Nov 2012].

4. USDA. Pesticide Data Program Annual Summary, Calendar Year 2010. Washington, DC: Agricultural Marketing Service, U.S. Department of Agriculture (May 2010). Available: http://www.ams.usda.gov/AMSv1.0/getfil?edDocName=stelprdc5098550 [accessed 14 Nov 2012].

5. Bouchard MF, et al. Prenatal exposure to organophosphate pesticides and IQ in 7-year-old children. Environ Health Perspect 119(8):1189–1195 (2011); http://dx.doi.org/10.1289/ehp.1003185.

6. Engel SM, et al. Prenatal exposure to organophosphates, paraoxonase 1, and cognitive development in childhood. Environ Health Perspect 119(8):1182–1188 (2011); http://dx.doi.org/10.1289/ehp.1003183.

7. Rauh V, et al. Seven-year neurodevelopmental scores and prenatal exposure to chlorpyrifos, a common agricultural pesticide. Environ Health Perspect 119(8):1196–1201 (2011); http://dx.doi.org/10.1289/ehp.1003160.

8. Bellinger DC. A strategy for comparing the contributions of environmental chemicals and other risk factors to neurodevelopment of children. Environ Health Perspect 120(4):501–507 (2012); http://dx.doi.org/10.1289/ehp.1104170.

9. Vandenberg LN, et al. Hormones and endocrine-disrupting chemicals: low-dose effects and nonmonotonic dose responses. Endocr Rev 33(3):378–455 (2012); http://dx.doi.org/10.1210/er.2011-1050.

10. Guerrero-Bosagna C, et al. Epigenetic transgenerational inheritance of vinclozolin induced mouse adult onset

disease and associated sperm epigenome biomarkers. Reprod Toxicol; http://dx.doi.org/10.1016/j.reprotox .2012.09.005 [online 2 Oct 2012].

11. Forman J, et al. Organic foods: health and environmental advantages and disadvantages. Pediatrics 130(5):e1406–e1415; http://dx.doi.org/10.1542/ peds.2012-2579.

Scared Fat: Are Consumers Being Scared Away from Healthy Foods?

SafeFruitsandVeggies.com

SafeFruitsandVeggies.com is a website published by the Alliance for Food and Farming, a nonprofit organization representing agriculture associations, commodity groups, and individual growers and shippers.

*A*re consumers being scared away from healthy foods?

It seems that scary stories about the foods we eat each day are becoming increasingly common in both traditional and social media channels. While the obvious end goal of the vast majority of the media is to provide the public with information that will help people choose healthy diets, a question that begs asking is if the Internet's growing appetite for content over substance might at times be causing the public to overreact and make unhealthy food choices? According to some experts, this indeed may be the case.

Recent data shows the percentage of Americans now classified as obese has risen above 40 percent and obesity rates among children are climbing distressingly fast. The causes of obesity are multifactorial in nature, however poor diet choices are widely accepted as one cause. In this regard, it is noteworthy that despite decades of public health education information, throughout America the average daily consumption of many healthy foods, such as fruits and vegetables, has been reported to be stagnant or declining. The identification of barriers to increasing fruit and vegetable consumption is an area of significant research in the public health community.

According to a recent consumer research study, it seems that for some consumers, fear and concern about the safety of fruits and vegetables may be having a negative impact on purchasing decisions at the grocery store and that activist groups who call certain fruits and vegetables "dirty" may be unintentionally impeding health initiatives like the First Lady's *Let's Move* campaign or the Produce for Better Health Foundation's *More Matters*. If fear continues to be a consumption barrier, how will Americans ever reach the USDA's new recommendation that half our plates be comprised of fruits and vegetables?

> *If a report . . . recommends that consumers choose organic options to lower their hypothetical "risk" of a myriad of cognitive disorders and diseases, the media should think twice before simply repeating the message.*

This important health issue was recently addressed by a group of experts in food safety, nutrition, farming and consumer behavior. This expert panel reviewed a new study conducted by the Charlton Research Group on behalf of the Alliance for Food and Farming, a non-profit group representing both conventional and organic fruit and vegetable farmers. The nationwide survey examined the potential impact of negative messages generated by activist groups that question the safety of fruits and vegetables and the impact of these messages on consumer attitudes towards buying fruits and vegetables. An analysis of this preliminary study suggests that concerns over the safety of fruits and vegetables are indeed influencing buyer behavior for some of the population. These research findings are similar to consumer research conducted previously by other organizations. The experts concluded there may be a growing public health threat caused by misinformation about food issues that people are exposed to through the media and the Internet. The panelists noted that reports focused on "potential risks" of some foods are rarely contrasted with information on the well-recognized benefits of these foods. The preliminary data presented in this report and in other ongoing studies, suggests that some consumers have decreased their intakes of fruits and vegetables out of concern that these foods may have pesticide residues. This action is clearly at odds with public health messages that increased consumption of fruits and vegetables is one way to reduce the risk for obesity. Regrettably, lack of balance in reporting on the health benefits versus risk of select foods can lead to consumer confusion and, potentially, lowering of faith in the government's ability to set guidelines that ensure safe food.

The expert panel agreed that consumers need more information from credible sources in order to make their shopping decisions. If a report advises consumers against eating certain kinds of fruits and vegetables or recommends that consumers choose organic options to lower their hypothetical "risk" of a myriad of cognitive disorders and diseases, the media should think twice before simply repeating the message. The expert panel noted these types of statements seem to have led a large portion of the population to believe that any level of pesticide on food presents a health risk. This contention does not represent the scientific consensus and it is not supported by comprehensive scientific studies. Rather, a multitude of studies conducted for decades show a wide-range of health benefits gained by eating diets rich in fruits and vegetables regardless if the products are grown conventionally or under organic conditions. What is not controversial is that one of the best things you can do for yourself and your family is to eat more fruits and vegetables.

A Stanford Study Found Pesticide Levels in Organic and Conventional Foods Within Safety Limits

Michelle Brandt

Michelle Brandt is the associate director of digital communications and media relations at Stanford University.

You're in the supermarket eyeing a basket of sweet, juicy plums. You reach for the conventionally grown stone fruit, then decide to spring the extra $1/pound for its organic cousin. You figure you've just made the healthier decision by choosing the organic product—but new findings from Stanford University cast some doubt on your thinking.

"There isn't much difference between organic and conventional foods, if you're an adult and making a decision based solely on your health," said Dena Bravata, MD, MS, the senior author of a paper comparing the nutrition of organic and non-organic foods, published in the Sept. 4 issue of *Annals of Internal Medicine*.

Little Difference between Organic and Conventional Foods

A team led by Bravata, a senior affiliate with Stanford's Center for Health Policy, and Crystal Smith-Spangler, MD, MS, an instructor in the school's Division of General Medical Disciplines and a physician-investigator at VA Palo Alto Health Care System, did the most comprehensive meta-analysis to date of existing studies comparing organic and conventional foods. They did not find strong evidence that organic foods are more nutritious or carry fewer health risks than conventional alternatives, though consumption of organic foods can reduce the risk of pesticide exposure.

The popularity of organic products, which are generally grown without synthetic pesticides or fertilizers or routine use of antibiotics or growth hormones, is skyrocketing in the United States. Between 1997 and 2011, U.S. sales of organic foods increased from $3.6 billion to $24.4 billion, and many consumers are willing to pay a premium for these products. Organic foods are often twice as expensive as their conventionally grown counterparts.

Although there is a common perception—perhaps based on price alone—that organic foods are better for you than non-organic ones, it remains an open question as to the health benefits. In fact, the Stanford study stemmed from Bravata's patients asking her again and again about the benefits of organic products. She didn't know how to advise them.

[Stanford University] researchers found little significant difference in health benefits between organic and conventional foods.

So Bravata, who is also chief medical officer at the health-care transparency company Castlight Health, did a literature search, uncovering what she called a "confusing body of studies, including some that were not very rigorous, appearing in trade publications." There wasn't a comprehensive synthesis of the evidence that included both benefits and harms, she said.

"This was a ripe area in which to do a systematic review," said first author Smith-Spangler, who jumped on board to conduct the meta-analysis with Bravata and other Stanford colleagues.

For their study, the researchers sifted through thousands of papers and identified 237 of the most relevant to analyze.

Those included 17 studies (six of which were randomized clinical trials) of populations consuming organic and conventional diets, and 223 studies that compared either the nutrient levels or the bacterial, fungal or pesticide contamination of various products (fruits, vegetables, grains, meats, milk, poultry, and eggs) grown organically and conventionally. There were no long-term studies of health outcomes of people consuming organic versus conventionally produced food; the duration of the studies involving human subjects ranged from two days to two years.

After analyzing the data, the researchers found little significant difference in health benefits between organic and conventional foods. No consistent differences were seen in the vitamin content of organic products, and only one nutrient—phosphorus—was significantly higher in organic versus conventionally grown produce (and the researchers note that because few people have phosphorous deficiency, this has little clinical significance). There was also no difference in protein or fat content between organic and conventional milk, though evidence from a limited number of studies suggested that organic milk may contain significantly higher levels of omega-3 fatty acids.

The researchers were also unable to identify specific fruits and vegetables for which organic appeared the consistently healthier choice, despite running what Bravata called "tons of analyses."

"Some believe that organic food is always healthier and more nutritious," said Smith-Spangler, who is also an instructor of medicine at the School of Medicine. "We were a little surprised that we didn't find that."

Safe Pesticide Levels

The review yielded scant evidence that conventional foods posed greater health risks than organic products. While researchers found that organic produce had a 30 percent lower risk of pesticide contamination than conventional fruits and vegetables, organic foods are not necessarily 100 percent free of pesticides. What's more, as the researchers noted, the pesticide levels of all foods generally fell within the allowable safety limits. Two studies of children consuming organic and conventional diets did find lower levels of pesticide residues in the urine of children on organic diets, though the significance of these findings on child health is unclear. Additionally, organic chicken and pork appeared to reduce exposure to antibiotic-resistant bacteria, but the clinical significance of this is also unclear.

As for what the findings mean for consumers, the researchers said their aim is to educate people, not to discourage them from making organic purchases. "If you look beyond health effects, there are plenty of other reasons to buy organic instead of conventional," noted Bravata. She listed taste preferences and concerns about the effects of conventional farming practices on the environment and animal welfare as some of the reasons people choose organic products.

"Our goal was to shed light on what the evidence is," said Smith-Spangler. "This is information that people can use to make their own decisions based on their level of concern about pesticides, their budget and other considerations."

She also said that people should aim for healthier diets overall. She emphasized the importance of eating fruits and vegetables, "however they are grown," noting that most Americans don't consume the recommended amount.

In discussing limitations of their work, the researchers noted the heterogeneity of the studies they reviewed due to differences in testing methods; physical factors affecting the food, such as weather and soil type; and great variation among organic farming methods. With regard to the latter, there may be specific organic practices (for example, the way that manure fertilizer, a risk for bacterial contamination, is used and handled) that could yield a safer product of higher nutritional quality.

"What I learned is there's a lot of variation between farming practices," said Smith-Spangler. "It appears there are a lot of different factors that are important in predicting nutritional quality and harms."

Are Lower Pesticides a Good Reason to Buy Organic? Probably Not

Christie Wilcox

Christie Wilcox is a science writer and blogger as well as a PhD student in cell and molecular biology at the University of Hawaii.

A lot of organic supporters are up in arms about the recent Stanford study that found no nutritional benefit to organic foods. Stanford missed the point, they say—it's not about what organic foods have in them, it's what they don't. After all, avoidance of pesticide residues is the #1 reason why people buy organic foods.

Yes, conventional foods have more synthetic pesticide residues than organic ones, on average. And yes, pesticides are dangerous chemicals. But does the science support paying significantly more for organic foods just to avoid synthetic pesticides? No.

A Pesticide Is a Pesticide

I'm not saying that pesticides, herbicides, and insect repellants aren't toxic. I certainly wouldn't recommend drinking cocktails laced with insect-repelling chemicals, for without a doubt, they can be bad for you. Pesticide exposure has been linked to all kinds of diseases and conditions, from neurodegenerative diseases like Parkinson's to cancer. What we do know, though, is that natural isn't synonymous with harmless. As a 2003 review of food safety concluded, "what should be made clear to consumers is that 'organic' does not equal 'safe.'"

I've said it before and I'll say it again: there is nothing safe about the chemicals used in organic agriculture. Period. This shouldn't be that shocking—after all, a pesticide is a pesticide. "Virtually all chemicals can be shown to be dangerous at high doses," explain scientists, "and this includes the thousands of natural chemicals that are consumed every day in food but most particularly in fruit and vegetables."

There's a reason we have an abundance of natural pesticides: plants and animals produce tens of thousands of chemicals to try and deter insects and herbivores from eating them. Most of these haven't been tested for their toxic potential, as the Reduced Risk Program of the US Environmental Protection Agency (EPA) applies to synthetic pesticides only. As more research is done into their toxicity, however, we find they are just as bad as synthetic pesticides, sometimes worse. Many natural pesticides have been found to be potential—or serious—health risks, including those used commonly in organic farming.

If you're going to worry about pesticides, worry about all of them, organic and synthetic.

In head-to-head comparisons, natural pesticides don't fare any better than synthetic ones. When I compared the organic chemicals copper sulfate and pyrethrum to the top synthetics, chlorpyrifos and chlorothalonil, I found that not only were the organic ones more acutely toxic, studies have found that they are more chronically toxic as well, and have higher negative impacts on non-target species. My results match with other scientific comparisons. In their recommendations to Parliament in 1999, the Committee on European Communities noted that copper sulfate, in particular, was far more dangerous than the synthetic alternative. A review of their findings can be seen in the table on the right [not shown] (from a recent review paper). Similarly, head-to-head comparisons have found that organic pesticides aren't better for the environment, either.

Organic pesticides pose the same health risks as non-organic ones. No matter what anyone tells you, organic pesticides don't just disappear. Rotenone is notorious for its lack of degradation, and copper sticks around for a long, long time. Studies have shown that copper sulfate, pyrethrins, and rotenone all can be detected on plants after harvest—for copper sulfate and rotenone, those levels exceeded safe limits. One study found such significant rotenone residues in olives and olive oil to warrant "serious doubts ... about the safety and healthiness of oils extracted from drupes treated with rotenone." Just like with certain synthetic pesticides, organic pesticide exposure has health implications—a study in Texas found that rotenone exposure correlated to a significantly higher risk of Parkinson's disease. The increased risk due to Rotenone was *five times higher* than the risk posed by the synthetic alternative, chlorpyrifos. Similarly, the FDA has known for a while that chronic exposure to copper sulfate can lead to anemia and liver disease.

So why do we keep hearing that organic foods have fewer pesticide residues? Well, because they have lower levels of *synthetic* pesticide residues. Most of our data on pesticide residues in food comes from surveys like the USDA's Pesticide Data Program (PDP). But while the PDP has been looking at the residues of over 300 pesticides in foods for decades, rotenone and copper sulfate aren't among the usual pesticides tested for—maybe, because for several organic pesticides, fast, reliable methods for detecting them were only developed recently. And, since there isn't any public data on the use of organic pesticides in organic farming (like there is for conventional farms), we're left guessing what levels of organic pesticides are on and in organic foods.

So, if you're going to worry about pesticides, worry about all of them, organic and synthetic. But, really, should you worry at all?

Systematic reviews of dietary pesticide exposure all come to the same conclusion: that typical dietary exposure to pesticide residues in foods poses minimal risks to humans.

You Are What You Eat? Maybe Not

We know, quite assuredly, that conventionally produced foods do contain higher levels of synthetic chemicals. But do these residues matter?

While study after study can find pesticide residues on foods, they are almost always well below safety standards. Almost all pesticides detected on foods by the USDA and independent scientific studies are at levels below 1% of the Acceptable Daily Intake (ADI) set by government regulators. This level isn't random—the ADI is based on animal exposure studies in a wide variety of species. First, scientists give animals different amounts of pesticides on a daily basis throughout their lifetimes and monitor those animals for toxic effects. Through this, they determine the highest dose at which no effects can be found. The ADI is then typically set 100 times *lower* than that level. So a typical human exposure that is 1% of the ADI is equivalent to an exposure 10,000 times lower than levels that are safe in animal models.

Systematic reviews of dietary pesticide exposure all come to the same conclusion: that typical dietary exposure to pesticide residues in foods poses minimal risks to humans. As the book *Health Benefits of Organic Food* explains, "while there is some evidence that consuming organic produce will lead to lower exposure of pesticides compared to the consumption of conventional produce, there is no evidence of effect at contemporary concentrations." Or, as a recent review states, "from a practical standpoint, the marginal benefits of reducing human exposure to pesticides in the diet through increased consumption of organic produce appear to be insignificant."

Reviews of the negative health effects of pesticides find that dangerous exposure levels don't come from food. Instead, non-dietary routes make for the vast majority of toxin exposures, in particular the use of pesticides around the home and workplace. A review of the worldwide disease burden caused by chemicals found that 70% can be attributed to air pollution, with acute poisonings and occupational exposures coming in second and third. Similarly, studies have found that indoor air concentrations of pesticides, not the amount on foodstuffs, correlate strongly to the amount of residues found in pregnant women (and even still, there was no strong correlation between exposure and health effects). Similarly, other studies have found that exposures to toxic pyrethroids come primarily from the environment. Children on organic diets routeinely had pyrethroids in their systems, and the organic group actually had higher levels of several pyrethroid metabolites than the conventional one. In other words, you have more to fear from your home than from your food.

Your home probably contains more pesticides than you ever imagined. Plastics and paints often contain fungicides to prevent mold—fungi that, by the way, can kill you. Your walls, carpets and floors also contain pesticides. Cleaning products and disinfectants contains pesticides and fungicides so they can do their job. Ever used an exterminator to get rid of mice, termites, fleas or cockroaches? That stuff can linger for months. Step outside your house, and just about everything you touch has come in contact with a pesticide. Insecticides are used in processing, manufacturing, and packaging, not to mention that even grocery stores use pesticide to keep insects and rodents at bay. These chemicals are all around you, every day, fighting off the pests that destroy our buildings and our food. It's not surprising that most pesticide exposures doesn't come from your food.

> To date, there is no scientific evidence that eating an organic diet leads to better health.

That said, there are some studies that have found a link between diet and exposure to specific pesticides, particularly synthetic organophosphorus pesticides. Lu et al. found that switching children from a conventional food diet to an entirely organic one dropped the urinary levels of specific metabolites for malathion and chlorpyrifos to nondetectable levels in a matter of days. But, it's important to note that even the levels they detected during the conventional diet are three orders of magnitude *lower* than the levels needed in animal experiments to cause neurodevelopmental or other adverse health effects.

While it might seem that decreasing exposure to pesticides in any way could only be good for you, toxicologists would differ. Contrary to what you might think, lower exposure isn't necessarily better. It's what's known as hormesis, or a hormetic dose response curve. There is evidence that exposure to most chemicals at doses significantly below danger thresholds, even pesticides, is beneficial when compared to no exposure at all. Why? Perhaps because it kick starts our immune system. Or, perhaps, because pesticides activate beneficial biological pathways. For most chemicals, we simply don't know. What we do know is that data collected from 5,000 dose response measurements (abstracted from over 20,000 studies) found that low doses of many supposedly toxic chemicals, metals, pesticides and fungicides either reduced cancer rates below controls or increased longevity or growth in a variety of animals. So while high acute and chronic exposures are bad, the levels we see in food that are well below danger thresholds may even be good for us. This isn't as surprising as you might think—just look at most pharmaceuticals. People take low doses of aspirin daily to improve their heart health, but at high chronic doses, it can cause anything from vomiting to seizures and even death. Similarly, a glass of red wine every day might be good for you. But ten glasses a day? Definitely not.

No Need to Fear

To date, there is no scientific evidence that eating an organic diet leads to better health.

What of all those studies I just mentioned linking pesticides to disorders? Well, exactly *none* of them looked at pesticides *from dietary intake* and health in people. Instead, they involve people with high occupational exposure (like farmers who spray pesticides) or household exposure (from gardening, etc). Judging the safety of dietary pesticide intake by high exposures is like judging the health impacts of red wine based on alcoholics. A systematic review of the literature found only three studies to date have looked at clinical outcomes of eating organic—and none found any difference between an organic and conventional diet. My question is: if organic foods are so much healthier, why aren't there any studies that show people on an organic diet are healthier than people eating conventionally grown produce instead?

More to the point, if conventional pesticide residues on food (and not other, high exposure routes) are leading to rampant disease, we should be able to find evidence of the connection in longitudinal epidemiological studies—but we don't. The epidemiological evidence for the danger of pesticide residues simply isn't there.

If dietary exposure to pesticides was a significant factor in cancer rates, we would expect to see that people who eat more conventionally grown fruits and vegetable have higher rates of cancer. But instead, we see the opposite. People who eat more fruits and vegetables have significantly lower incidences of cancers, and those who eat the most are two times less likely to develop cancer than those who eat the least. While high doses of pesticides over time have been linked to cancer in lab animals and *in vitro* studies, "epidemiological studies do not support the idea that synthetic pesticide residues are important for human cancer." Even the exposure to the persistent and villainized pesticide DDT has not been consistently linked to cancer. As a recent review of the literature summarized, "no hard evidence currently exists that toxic hazards such as pesticides have had a major impact on total cancer incidence and mortality, and this is especially true for diet-related exposures."

The focus on pesticides is misleading, as pesticide residues are the lowest food hazard when it comes to human health.

The closest we have to studying the effects of diet on health are studies looking at farmers. However, farmers in general have high occupational pesticide exposures, and thus it's impossible to tease out occupational versus dietary exposure. Even still, in this high-risk group, studies simply don't find health differences between organic and conventional farmers. A UK study found that conventional farmers were just as healthy as organic ones, though the organic ones were happier. Similarly, while test-tube studies of high levels of pesticides are known to cause reproductive disorders, a comparison of sperm quality from organic and conventional farmers was unable to connect dietary intake of over 40 different pesticides to any kind of reproductive impairment. Instead, the two groups showed no statistical difference in their sperm quality.

In a review of the evidence for choosing organic food, Christine Williams said it simply: "There are virtually no studies of any size that have evaluated the effects of organic v.

conventionally-grown foods." Thus, she explains, "conclusions cannot be drawn regarding potentially beneficial or adverse nutritional consequences, to the consumer, of increased consumption of organic food."

"There is currently no evidence to support or refute claims that organic food is safer and thus, healthier, than conventional food, or vice versa. Assertions of such kind are inappropriate and not justified," explain scientists. Neither organic nor conventional food is dangerous to eat, they say, and the constant attention to safety is unwarranted. Worse, it does more harm than good. The scientists chastise the media and industry alike for scaremongering tactics, saying that "the selective and partial presentation of evidence serves no useful purpose and does not promote public health. Rather, it raises fears about unsafe food."

Furthermore, the focus on pesticides is misleading, as pesticide residues are the lowest food hazard when it comes to human health. . . . They conclude that as far as the scientific evidence is concerned, "it seems that other factors, if any, rather than safety aspects speak in favor of organic food."

If you don't want to listen to those people or me, listen to the toxicologists, who study this stuff for a living. When probed about the risk that different toxins pose, over 85% rejected the notion that organic or "natural" products are safer than others. They felt that smoking, sun exposure and mercury were of much higher concern than pesticides. Over 90% agreed that the media does a terrible job of reporting about toxic substances, mostly by overstating the risks. They slammed down hard on non-governmental organizations, too, for overstating risk.

What's in a Name?

There's good reason we can't detect differences between organic and conventional diets: the labels don't mean that much. Sure, organic farms have to follow a certain set of USDA guidelines, but farm to farm variability is huge for both conventional and organic practices. As a review of organic practices concluded: "variation within organic and conventional farming systems is likely as large as differences between the two systems."

The false dichotomy between conventional and organic isn't just misleading, it's dangerous. Our constant attention to natural versus synthetic only causes fear and distrust, when in actuality, our food has never been safer. Eating less fruits and vegetables due to fear of pesticides or the high price of organics does far more harm to our health than any of the pesticide residues on our food.

Let me be clear about one thing: I'm all for reducing pesticide use. But we can't forget that pesticides are used for a reason, too. We have been reaping the rewards of pesticide use for decades. Higher yields due to less crop destruction. Safer food because of reduced fungal and bacterial contamination. Lower prices as a result of increased supply and longer shelf life. Protection from pests that carry deadly diseases. Invasive species control, saving billions of dollars in damages—and the list goes on. Yes, we need to manage the way we use pesticides, scrutinize the chemicals involved and monitor their effects to ensure safety, and Big Ag (conventional and organic) needs to be kept in check. But without a doubt, our lives have been vastly improved by the chemicals we so quickly villainize.

If we want to achieve the balance between sustainability, production outputs, and health benefits, we have to stop focusing on brand names. Instead of emphasizing labels, we need to look at different farming practices and the chemicals involved and judge them independently of whether they fall under organic standards.

In the meantime, buy fresh, locally farmed produce, whether it's organic or not; if you can talk to the farmers, you'll know exactly what is and isn't on your food. Wash it well, and you'll get rid of most of whatever pesticides are on there, organic or synthetic. And eat lots and lots of fruits and vegetables—if there is anything that will improve your health, it's that.

Before you say otherwise and get mad at me for mentioning it, rotenone is currently a USDA approved organic pesticide. It was temporarily banned, but reapproved in 2010. Before it was banned, it was the most commonly used organic pesticide, and now—well, without public data on pesticide use on organic farms, we have no idea how much it is being used today.

CHAPTER 2

How Are Pesticides Affecting the Environment?

Chapter Preface

One of the most well-known pesticides is DDT (dichlorodiphenyltrichloroethane)—an organochlorine insecticide that was once promoted as a revolutionary solution to a variety of insect problems. DDT soon fell into disfavor, however, when it was found to be highly toxic to both the environment and human health. The story of DDT unfolded during and following World War II—a period when the power of chemistry was just beginning to be understood. It marked the birth of the pesticide industry, and many commentators say it stands today as a warning about the danger of unleashing toxic chemicals before they are fully understood.

DDT was the brainchild of a German chemist, Paul Hermann Müller. In 1939, Müller's pesticide research led to the discovery of a synthetic chlorinated hydrocarbon that he called DDT. After Müller found that the DDT was effective at killing houseflies, he worked to make it an even more potent insecticide. Müller soon realized that DDT was the best insecticide ever invented—small amounts of DDT instantly killed a wide range of insects yet it seemed to have no negative effects on humans. Müller obtained a patent for DDT as an insecticide and manufacturing began.

During World War II, DDT was employed by British and American militaries to control deadly diseases, such as typhus, malaria, typhoid, and dysentery, that were threatening Allied soldiers around the world. A new insecticide was a thrilling prospect at that point in history because the Allies needed a substitute for pyrethrum, a natural pesticide historically used to combat insects that was no longer available from Japan, an enemy nation. Military field tests of DDT in 1943 successfully stopped typhus epidemics in Mexico, Algeria, Egypt, and Italy, and DDT was also excellent at destroying lice—a problem that plagued soldiers and war refugees alike. Soon American soldiers and sailors were issued cans of DDT to spray tents, barracks, and mess halls to rid them of harmful insects and prevent disease. DDT was especially valued in tropical locations, but it was also heavily used by the European militaries and in European refugee camps. By the war's end, DDT was viewed by people around the world as a great invention. In 1948, in fact, Müller was awarded a Nobel Prize in Medicine for his discovery of the insecticidal qualities of DDT.

After the war ended, private industry in the United States rushed to manufacture DDT for use in US homes, yards, and commercial agriculture. DDT was also in great demand for insect control in tropical areas, and even in American southern states, to prevent malaria and other insect-borne diseases. For a while, DDT seemed to fulfill its early promise. During the 1950s malaria infections were reduced worldwide and farm production was increased as much as 40 percent, providing food for many starving people in the post-war period.

By the late 1950s and early 1960s, however, scientists began to question the safety of DDT for both the environment and human health. DDT was so effective that it often wiped out all insects and birds in a sprayed area, and this impact often upset the ecological balance in ways that allowed other unwanted pests to proliferate. Part of the reason for DDT's spectacular effectiveness was the fact that it was not soluble in water, so rain did not wash it off. That meant that it was persistent in the environment, so that year after year it built up in fields, orchards, forests, yards, and everywhere it was sprayed. Biologists and other observers soon noticed the decline of certain species that coincided with the heavy use of DDT. Bald eagles, for example, were no longer breeding in some parts of the United States, and in other areas eagle egg shells were too thin to produce offspring. Similar declines were seen in peregrine falcons, ospreys, and other birds around the globe, and DDT was found to be at fault. DDT was even detected in the world's oceans and in Antarctica, where seals, penguins, and carnivores were all found to carry residues of DDT.

In 1962, the publication of a book, *Silent Spring*, by American biologist Rachel Carson, helped to publicize the threat of DDT and other toxic pesticides. Carson's book highlighted the dangers of DDT to both the environment and humans, and warned of a possible disastrous breakdown of the ocean and other global ecosystems if such pesticides continued to be used. Carson was severly criticized by the pesticide industry, but President John F. Kennedy appointed a science advisory committee that recommended that DDT use be immediately reduced and eliminated completely as soon as possible. Over the next few years, the federal government and many states began banning the chemical for many uses, and in 1972 the newly created US Environmental Protection Agency (EPA) instituted a total ban on the pesticide in the United States. EPA cited the negative environmental effects of DDT and its potentially serious human health effects as the basis of its decision. Since then, additional research has shown DDT to be a probable cause of human reproductive problems, such as male infertility, miscarriages, and low birth weight, as well as a human carcinogen that can lead to breast and other cancers, nervous system problems, and liver damage. Today, DDT residues in the environment have decreased but are still a cause for concern in some areas.

Although DDT was banned worldwide for agricultural uses by the 2001 Stockholm Convention on Persistent Organic Pollutants, an exemption was made for DDT to be used by some developing countries because it is both cheap and effective, and often the only pesticide these poor countries could afford. In 2006 the World Health Organization (WHO) endorsed the use of DDT in African and Asian countries where malaria continues to be a deadly and widespread problem. Since then, the use of DDT in these countries has been increasing. There continues to be debate about this, however, because environmentalists want to see a total global ban, while some groups involved in global health initiatives promote an expansion of DDT usage.

Many new pesticides have been introduced since the time of DDT's discovery, some of them equally toxic, according to health and environment experts. This chapter includes viewpoints describing the many different impacts of pesticides on the natural environment.

Environmental Impacts

Pesticide Action Network North America

Pesticide Action Network North America (PANNA) is an advocacy organization that works to replace the use of hazardous pesticides with ecologically sound and socially responsible alternatives.

When chemicals that are designed to kill are introduced into delicately balanced ecosystems, they can set damage in motion that reverberates through the food web for years.

- Honeybee populations are plummeting nationwide.
- Male frogs exposed to atrazine become females.
- Pesticides are implicated in dramatic bat die-offs.

Pesticides wreak havoc on the environment, threatening biodiversity and weakening the natural systems upon which human survival depends. PAN works hard to promote agricultural systems that protect and strengthen, rather than contaminate, our natural ecosystems.

Bees, Bats and Frogs Dying Off in Droves

Five great extinction events have reshaped earth in the past 439 million years, each wiping out between half and 95% of planetary life. The most recent was the killing off of dinosaurs. Today, we're living through a sixth great cataclysm. Seven in ten biologists believe that mass extinction poses an even greater threat to humanity than the global warming which contributes to it.

Amphibians were the first to start dying off—in 1998 scientists identified the cause as a type of fungus, with population declines showing a strong correlation to pesticide exposure. A few years later America's honeybees started dying—populations have dropped by 29%–36% each year since 2006 (see below).

Without bees, say goodbye to almonds, peaches—even chocolate. Fully 1/3 of the food we eat depends on bees for pollination.

Bee populations have dropped 30% per year since 2006.

Bats are the most recent victims. In 2006 the first cave floors were found covered with dead bats in the Northeast. Some scientists believe that like amphibians, bats have become more susceptible to deadly disease (in this case, White Nose Syndrome) because their immune systems are weakened by pesticides. A growing body of evidence points towards pesticide exposure—even at so-called "safe levels"—as a key contributor to these and other problems for wildlife.

Mystery of Disappearing Honeybees

Without bees, say goodbye to almonds, peaches—even chocolate. Fully 1/3 of the food we eat depends on bees for pollination. So when the insects suddenly started dying off and abandoning their hives in 2006, scientists, beekeepers and farmers sounded the alarm. Researchers dubbed the phenomenon "Colony Collapse Disorder," and went to work trying to find a cause.

As scientists unravel the mystery, they are discovering that exposure to pesticides—perhaps acting in synergy with other stressors—is a prime suspect. Most insecticides are inherently toxic to bees, and a recent study found a cocktail of toxic pesticides in the wax and honey of commercial hives. A new class of insecticides called neonicotinoids has been specifically implicated.

Some U.S. beekeepers are responding by keeping their hives away from crops where these pesticides are used. Many European countries, including France, Germany, Italy and Slovenia, have already banned neonicotinoids in response to the threat, and beekeepers in these countries report that hives are beginning to recover. Meanwhile, researchers in the U.S. have established a Colony Collapse Disorder Working Group, as farmers and beekeepers anxiously await solutions.

Male Tadpoles Become Females in Contaminated Water

What do you call a weed killer that can give a frog a sex change? Its primary manufacturer, Syngenta, calls it "Aatrex", but it's commonly known as atrazine. More than 75 million pounds of the herbicide are used on U.S. farms every year, making it the second most-used pesticide in agriculture. And it contaminates water supplies throughout the Midwest at levels above those found to turn male tadpoles into female frogs in the lab.

In the 1990s, the Syngenta corporation funded Dr. Tyrone Hayes of UC Berkeley to study the environmental impacts of atrazine. When Dr. Hayes discovered ovaries growing in the testes of male frogs raised in atrazine-contaminated water, Syngenta refused to let him publish his findings. Hayes repeated the experiment with independent funding, and today continues research on atrazine's dramatic impacts on amphibians.

Atrazine's effect on amphibians is shocking: 10% of male frogs raised in atrazine-laced water developed into females. Genetically, the frogs are still males, but morphologically they are completely female—they can even mate successfully with other males and lay viable eggs.

Switzerland, where Syngenta is based, banned atrazine in 2001. EPA officials are currently reviewing the chemical's use in the U.S. PAN and our Midwest partners are pressing hard for transparent, science-based decisionmaking without undue influence from Syngenta—the largest chemical company in the world.

Fouled Waterways Endanger Fish and Birds

Some pesticides seep through the soil into groundwater; others are washed by rain into creeks, rivers, and lakes where they can poison fish and other aquatic organisms. Depending on the type of chemical, contamination can last for days, weeks, months—even decades.

- *California*: Pesticides used by homeowners on lawns poison invertebrates at the bottom of aquatic food chains, upsetting fragile ecosystems statewide.

- *Florida Everglades*: Endosulfan runoff from tomato fields threatens the small fish that feed ibises, storks, and egrets.

Pesticide runoff remains largely unregulated, and government agencies have shown little initiative in protecting complex aquatic ecosystems. Fortunately, when tainted runoff threatens a species already listed as endangered, the government can be forced to act. In the pacific northwest, creeks that are home to endangered salmon now require substantial buffer zones from toxic pesticides. The Center for Biological Diversity recently took legal action to force EPA to protect 887 threatened and endangered species from 400 of the most dangerous pesticides.

Source URL: http://www.panna.org/issues/persistent -poisons/environmental-impacts

Water Pollution from Farming Is Worsening, Costing Billions

Tara Patel

Tara Patel is a reporter for Bloomberg News, a worldwide news organization.

Water pollution from agriculture is costing billions of dollars a year in developed countries and is set to rise in China and India as farmers race to increase food production, the Organization for Economic Cooperation and Development [OECD] said.

"Pollution from farm pesticides and fertilizers is often diffuse, making it hard to pin down exactly where it's coming from," Kevin Parris, author of a report by the Paris-based organization, said in an interview in Marseille. "In some big agricultural countries in Europe, like parts of France, Spain and the U.K. [United Kingdom], the situation is deteriorating."

In some regions of China, pollution of waterways from agriculture may already have reached a level that may cause health problems in humans, he said.

The OECD report is part of a series of studies published this week to coincide with the World Water Forum in Marseille. Ministers, industry representatives and non-government organizations are discussing resource management, waste, health risks and climate change at the meeting. Pollution from farming is gaining prominence as the global population increases, raising demand for food and putting strain on water resources.

Fertilizers such as nitrates and phosphates as well as pesticides that run off farms can contaminate drinking water, harm aquatic life and result in eutrophication, or a proliferation of plants that reduces oxygen content in water and eliminates other sea life, according to the study.

Lakes at Risk

"The number of lakes at risk of harmful algal blooms will increase by 20 percent in the first half of this century," the OECD said. By 2050 the nitrogen surpluses per hectare from agriculture are forecast to drop in OECD member countries and rise in China and India.

Costs from agricultural pollution include money spent treating water to remove nitrates, phosphates and pesticide chemicals as well as paying farmers to store manure safely and block contamination from reaching waterways, according to the study. Environmental contamination such as algal blooms also adds to the bill.

Beaches covered in green algae are becoming an annual occurrence in Brittany, France's westernmost region. The issue pits the region's 3.6 billion-euro ($4.7 billion) tourism industry against its 8.2 billion-euro [$6.3 billion] farming sector, whose large quantities of animal waste and use of fertilizers are blamed by scientists for feeding the so-called green tides that form in Brittany's shallow bays.

"Not Going Away"

"This is big and it's not going away," Parris said, referring to massive blooms in regions around the world including the Gulf of Mexico. "Regulations exist but they are often not enforced."

In Australia, the cost of algal blooms may be as high as $155 million while the price of eutrophication of surface and coast waters in France could reach as much as $1.4 billion, according to the study. Freshwater eutrophication costs are estimated at $2.2 billion in the U.S. and $2 billion for pesticide contamination of groundwater.

"In China there is already a chronic problem as well as in parts of India," Parris said. Worldwide researchers aren't getting the full picture of pollution from farming because access to data is incomplete.

The OECD study also highlights possible health risks from so-called "emerging water contaminants" from agriculture such as veterinary medicines used to treat livestock and substances created from pesticides when they are transformed in the environment.

"The impact of these mixtures is likely to be greater than the impact of the single substance on its own," the report said.

Pesticides Have Been Linked to Honeybee Decline

Karen Feldscher

Karen Feldscher is a senior writer/project manager at the Harvard School of Public Health.

The likely culprit in sharp worldwide declines in honeybee colonies since 2006 is imidacloprid, one of the most widely used pesticides, according to a new study from the Harvard School of Public Health (HSPH).

The authors, led by Alex Lu, associate professor of environmental exposure biology in the Department of Environmental Health, write that the new research provides "convincing evidence" of the link between imidacloprid and the phenomenon known as Colony Collapse Disorder (CCD), in which adult bees abandon their hives.

The study will appear in the June [2012] issue of the *Bulletin of Insectology*.

A Crucial Discovery

"The significance of bees to agriculture cannot be underestimated," says Lu. "And it apparently doesn't take much of the pesticide to affect the bees. Our experiment included pesticide amounts below what is normally present in the environment."

Pinpointing the cause of the problem is crucial because bees—beyond producing honey—are prime pollinators of roughly one-third of the crop species in the United States, including fruits, vegetables, nuts, and livestock feed such as alfalfa and clover. Massive loss of honeybees could result in billions of dollars in agricultural losses, experts estimate.

Lu and his co-authors hypothesized that the uptick in CCD resulted from the presence of imidacloprid, a neonicotinoid introduced in the early 1990s. Bees can be exposed in two ways: through nectar from plants or through high-fructose corn syrup beekeepers use to feed their bees. (Since most U.S.-grown corn has been treated with imidacloprid, it's also found in corn syrup.)

> *Strikingly ... it took only low levels of imidacloprid to cause hive collapse—less than what is typically used in crops or in areas where bees forage.*

Low Levels of Imidacloprid

In the summer of 2010, the researchers conducted an *in situ* study in Worcester County aimed at replicating how imidacloprid may have caused the CCD outbreak. Over a 23-week period, they monitored bees in four different bee yards; each yard had four hives treated with different levels of imidacloprid and one control hive. After 12 weeks of imidacloprid dosing, all the bees were alive. But after 23 weeks, 15 of the 16 imidacloprid-treated hives had perished. Those exposed to the highest levels of the pesticide died first.

The characteristics of the dead hives were consistent with CCD, said Lu; the hives were empty except for food stores, some pollen, and young bees, with few dead bees nearby. When other conditions cause hive collapse—such as disease or pests—many dead bees are typically found inside and outside the affected hives.

Strikingly, said Lu, it took only low levels of imidacloprid to cause hive collapse—less than what is typically used in crops or in areas where bees forage.

Scientists, policymakers, farmers, and beekeepers, alarmed at the sudden losses of between 30 percent and 90 percent of honeybee colonies since 2006, have posed numerous theories as to the cause of the collapse, including pests, disease, pesticides, migratory beekeeping, or some combination of these factors.

Pesticide Drift Is Damaging Organic Crops and Harming People

Clare Howard

Clare Howard is a freelance journalist and member of 100 Reporters, an online news site.

Brian and Anita Poeppel were brimming with excitement when they left their farm just outside Chicago and moved to 15 acres they planned to farm organically in Central Illinois. Trouble started before the first harvest. It was invisible, sometimes drifting into the big old farmhouse on a summer breeze, sometimes blanketing the children's backyard swing set, always teasing with its anonymity and guile.

The Poeppels had known from the beginning theirs would be an organic farm surrounded by a sea of farms using chemical fertilizers and pesticides. To the young couple, it had at first seemed reasonable that organic farmers and chemical farmers could coexist. The Poeppels visited their new neighbors and talked about their hopes and dreams of a healthy life.

For six years, the couple struggled when pesticides sprayed on nearby farms drifted over their property. Their daughters stayed indoors gazing out at their swing set, wading pool and favorite climbing trees. Once, Brian Poeppel, 40, was arrested for trespass. He had tried to block a chemical applicator working on a nearby field, saying the pesticides were blowing directly onto the Poeppel's property. He was convicted of disorderly conduct, fined $500 and put on probation for two years.

Then the Poeppels changed their strategy. They stopped pleading with neighbors, and started filing complaints with the Illinois Department of Agriculture. They organized a state-wide network of farmers to investigate pesticide drift. The Poeppels signed up for the Drift Catcher program conducted by the Pesticide Action Network [PAN], a not-for-profit group. Organic farmers 2,000 miles west of them organized a movement they are calling the Pitchfork Rebellion, and turned to independent urinalysis testing.

Their independent analysis is producing a startling picture of the tendency of pesticides sprayed in one area to migrate on the air and in water supplies. Along with new research on the potential health effects of these chemicals, these analyses are prompting a new vision of chemical drift as a form of trespass, willful negligence and property damage.

"The system is phenomenally productive with huge yields, small amounts of work and little fossil fuel input," said Dave Kennell, associate director of the Center for Renewable Energy at Illinois State University. "But now we know about the dead zones (in oceans), human health effects, death of the soil, erosion and resistant pathogens and weeds.

"We can't discount that when we look at the big picture," Kennell said.

Spray drift in the form of droplets or dust that moves off the targeted site is regulated, but . . . drift that has volatilized, or turned to vapor, is unregulated by the EPA.

A French court issued a historic verdict finding biotech giant Monsanto guilty of pesticide poisoning of a 47-year-old French grain farmer who suffered neurological damage including memory loss, headaches and stammering after a 2004 incident when he inhaled the herbicide Lasso, a product banned in the European Union in 2007 but still registered and used in the United States.

In a statement, the company said it had complied with safety and marketing guidelines in force at the time, and that it plans to appeal.

Gathering Evidence

On a Sunday in July, already hot and humid by mid-morning, two other organic farm families joined the Poeppels for a training session to learn how to install and operate Drift Catcher monitoring equipment. Karl Tupper, then a scientist with PAN, flew from California to conduct the training. Organic farmers Greg and Janet Morse rumbled into the barnyard on their 1980 Honda motorcycle. Jane Heim drove down from her farm near Paw Paw, Ill.

Training started in the barn with a PowerPoint presentation projected onto a white sheet hung from the rafters. In other regions of the country, Tupper told the group, evidence gathered through Drift Catchers helped shape public policy. He explained that spray drift in the form of droplets or dust that moves off the targeted site is regulated, but that drift that has volatilized, or turned to vapor, is unregulated by the EPA [US Environmental Protection Agency] and by state agencies. Drift Catcher monitoring equipment detects both types.

Laboratory analysis of results from each farm can cost more than $6,000.

The [Morses worry] that after years of effort and expense to earn the U.S. Certified Organic designation for their farm, they could lose their status because of drift.

"This country has built an agricultural economy around toxins," Tupper said. "These pesticides are in our bodies. Drift is inevitable. But the chemical industry wants to say drift is okay as long as it is below some safe amount.

"How do you define that safe amount, especially when a profit is made from these chemicals, but the cost of drift falls on the victim?" Tupper asked.

The Morses have farmed 365 acres without chemicals for 23 years in the Crow Creek valley near Putnam, Ill., and say they have fought all that time against chemical drift. In 1999, they said, spray drift damage covered their entire farm. But the source was not clear. The couple worries that after years of effort and expense to earn the U.S. Certified Organic designation for their farm, they could lose their status because of drift.

Greg Morse and his wife continue to file complaints even though little is done. They said they face regular retaliation, insisting that spray planes working on nearby farms often buzz their house. They took extra precautions when their children were growing up. They feared their son, a long-distance track runner who often ran through their timberland, would be deliberately sprayed as retaliation for his parents' complaints.

"One time, I just went berserk when a plane buzzed our house and turned on the sprayer over our farm," said Morse, 64. "I took a shotgun and play acted. There was no shell in the gun. A Putnam County sheriff came out to the farm and said he'd heard I was shooting at crop planes. But we're in Bureau County, so within three hours a Bureau County Sheriff shows up."

Asked about the incident, Bureau County Sheriff John Thompson said his deputy responded to a complaint filed by the plane pilot, a transient crop duster.

But Sheriff Thompson added that pesticide drift is a common problem. He rides his motorcycle to work and has been sprayed by a crop duster.

"I have no idea what the chemicals were," he said.

The Morses point to the irony of this. When they file drift complaints with the Illinois Department of Agriculture, it can be weeks before an inspector shows up to investigate and take samples for chemical residue. One time, Greg Morse was standing in his pasture with his organic cows and felt the chemical spray dousing him.

"I can't afford to have a camera crew filming these guys. It shouldn't be up to us to monitor all the time. Why should we have to regulate and defend?" he asked.

Tupper, of the Pesticide Action Network, is sympathetic but said, "The onus falls on the victim."

The government subsidizes farmers of chemically-treated commodity crops including corn, cotton, soybeans and wheat. There is no subsidy program for organic produce.

"Not only are we the victims," Brian Poeppel said, "but we're the bad guys in the community just because we don't want to be drifted on."

Chemical manufacturers contend their products pose no hazards. In a statement late Tuesday, Syngenta, which manufactures the weed-killer atrazine, dismissed concerns about its safety. Some 76 million pounds of atrazine are applied over American soil each year, much of it aerially.

The company called atrazine "one of the most carefully examined herbicides in the world," adding, "Its safety has been clearly established by more than 6,000 scientific studies conducted over the past 50 years."

Under the U.S. Farm Bill, the government subsidizes farmers of chemically-treated commodity crops including corn, cotton, soybeans and wheat. There is no subsidy program for organic produce.

"It looks like the government is on the chemical industry's side," said Janet Morse, 62.

People get discouraged from filing complaints because the government does not enforce regulations, Anita Poeppel said.

"Campaign to get people to report drift," Tupper said. "When complaints are not filed, agencies say there is no problem. Slowly but surely things are changing. Buffer zones and no-spray zones are being established."

After lunch under the backyard maple trees, the group unpacked and assembled the monitoring equipment. Everyone had a hand at putting together the equipment and reviewing recording procedures. It was a long, humid day with little levity save that provided by Bella, the Poeppel's Anatolian shepherd, who liked to be either in the thick of things or running through the children's wading pool.

Everyone passed certification in the Drift Catcher program. By late afternoon, Janet Morse stood alone, staring at the assembled equipment.

"I've been waiting for this for 23 years," she said quietly, almost to herself.

The Results

Results came back five months later, just days before Thanksgiving. The Poeppel and Morse farms were getting chlorpyrifos drift, an insecticide considered highly toxic to bees, wildlife and humans even at low levels. It is used widely on corn. The EPA banned all uses in homes and daycare centers because of its toxicity for children, but still allows its agricultural uses. Chlorpyrifos is linked to ADHD [attention deficit hyperactivity disorder] and autism, is considered hazardous to brain development and impacts neurobehavioral development in fetuses and children. In utero exposure at even minor levels is linked with pervasive developmental disorders.

The highest concentration of chlorpyrifos detected was at the Poeppel farm. The Drift Catcher log at the time of the sampling included a notation that pesticides were being applied by plane several miles to the northwest.

Dr. Susan Kegley, a scientist who founded the Pesticide Research Institute in 2006 to provide research and consulting on the chemistry of pesticides, considers this alarming for several reasons. The distance between the Poeppel farm and the aerial application was about two miles or more, yet drift was still detected. The level was about half the EPA recommended exposure limit for a 1-year-old child; however, because the reading was an average over a 20-hour period, there could have been dangerous spikes. She believes neurological harm can be occurring at levels lower than what the EPA considers safe.

"This is a pesticide that should be taken off the market. We can't afford to have more children with ADHD and developmental problems," she said. "The EPA has not included inhalation of chlorpyrifos in its risk assessment, believing it's not significant. We found inhalation is a huge risk for people living near an application."

For the Poeppels, the level of chlorpyrifos confirms their suspicions, but reopens the question of whether to stay or sell the farm and try to start somewhere else.

"We're getting blasted. We're right in the middle of this and we fear for our girls—raising them in this area," Anita Poeppel said. "Whenever we ask someone about what is being aerially applied, they say, 'Don't worry, it's just fungicide.'"

Now they are striking at the pocketbooks of neighbors who use aerial spraying, by filing claims to their insurance companies. Their first claim is being processed. An inspector came to the farm and confirmed what the Poeppels knew: the organic apple crop had been damaged by chemical drift.

Pesticides May Not Be Effective at Eliminating West Nile Virus

Lynne Peeples

Lynne Peeples is a reporter who covers the environment and public health at The Huffington Post, *an online news and analysis website.*

Massachusetts boasted a 60 percent kill rate. Vermont claimed up to 69 percent. And, in Texas, a preliminary report suggested that aerial spraying of pesticides eliminated 93 percent of disease-carrying mosquitoes in some neighborhoods.

Over the last couple months [2012], officials from across the country have engaged airplanes armed with pesticides in an attempt to battle mosquitoes that carry the West Nile virus, on track to infect more people this year than ever before in the U.S., and eastern equine encephalitis, a less common but generally more dangerous disease. The decisions to spray have often been made under heated opposition from residents and some scientists concerned about what they say is an ineffective and unsafe strategy. Nevertheless, in at least a few cases, officials subsequently reported high success rates and few health complaints.

"This is what we hoped to see. It's a meaningful reduction," said Roger Nasci, chief of the arboviral diseases branch of the U.S. Centers for Disease Control and Prevention, referring to very preliminary data from Dallas that suggested mosquito kills as high as 93 percent from aerial sprays in late August. "All things together, no one is going to say it is 100 percent positively safe. But the level of concern for risks to human health is low and certainly outweighed by the risk of West Nile."

Skeptism about Pesticide Success

Some remain skeptical, going as far as to threaten legal action.

"I don't believe those figures. Frankly, I don't think they're real," said David Pimentel, an emeritus professor at Cornell University, when shown the reported kill numbers from Massachusetts, Vermont and Texas. "I've done enough to know that it's not easy to kill those little devils. And measuring the kill of mosquitoes is not easy to do."

[One researcher] has found that up to 90 percent of an aerial spray misses the target and drifts away into the environment, poisoning beneficial insects such as bees.

Kyla Bennett, director of the non-profit New England Public Employees for Environmental Responsibility, acted on her doubts. On Aug. 8, after reading a press release that reported July aerial sprays across nearly 500,000 acres of southeastern Massachusetts had killed approximately 60 percent of eastern equine encephalitis-carrying mosquitoes, she filed a public records request for the supporting data. Two weeks later, on Aug. 22, she appealed to the state, noting that she had not yet received any records backing up the kill claim. A response from the state supervisor of records arrived in her mailbox Monday, saying the Department of Public Health is "identifying records responsive" to her request.

"How hard could it be to search for that data? It should be at their fingertips if they issued this press release," said Bennett, a former U.S. Environmental Protection Agency [EPA] worker who lives in southeastern Massachusetts. "This makes me even more suspicious that the 60 percent number isn't accurate.

"We are thinking of taking legal action at this point," Bennett added.

The *Huffington Post* also filed a formal public records request for the data on Monday, after being repeatedly told by the state Department of Public Health they had no one available to speak.

"It is important to know how these numbers were generated," said Jay Feldman, executive director of the non-profit Beyond Pesticides. "The burden is on the regulator to show that there is efficacy. The data that is available calls that into question."

Some of the data questioning aerial spraying's effectiveness comes from the research of Cornell's Pimentel, who has found that up to 90 percent of an aerial spray misses the target and drifts away into the environment, poisoning beneficial insects such as bees.

Under ideal conditions—with few trees to block the chemicals' descent and calm weather—Pimentel suggested it might be possible to kill 60 percent of the mosquitoes. Southeastern Massachusetts is heavily wooded and Pimentel added that any success may be short-lived given the short life cycle of the mosquito. Post-spray mosquito counts around Dallas, for example, were generally completed within a day or two and compared with counts from the weeks prior to the spray.

Some individuals who oppose spraying have also raised concerns that exposure to even minute doses of the EPA-approved pesticides used in aerial spraying could pose risks to human health.

Further, Pimentel said he is concerned that spraying contributes to the development of pesticide resistance in mosquitoes, which may lead to less successful efforts against mosquito-borne diseases in the future. As *HuffPost* previously reported, this issue is being addressed by California officials, who added more toxic pesticides to their aerial spray cocktail this year.

Charles Apperson, a public health entomologist at North Carolina State University, said he is less concerned. "If you make repeated sprays over years, there is potential for resistant populations to develop," he said, referencing the well-known resistance resulting from the ongoing use of pesticides in Africa to combat malaria. "But in a place like Dallas, where they hardly ever spray, there is not much danger of resistance."

As for the effectiveness of aerial spraying, Apperson noted that it is highly variable. "People against spraying can sure find instances where it doesn't work," he said. "But there are a lot of instances where it does work."

Some individuals who oppose spraying have also raised concerns that exposure to even minute doses of the EPA-approved pesticides used in aerial spraying could pose risks to human health, from asthma attacks to hormone problems. At particular risk, they say, are children.

"I am worried," said Vanessa Van Gilder of Dallas, who launched a Change.org petition opposing the aerial spraying that, as of Tuesday, had accumulated 2,127 signatures. "How many times have they told us something was safe and then 10 years later it comes out that it's not safe?"

While Nasci and Apperson said they doubt any meaning-ful health risks are posed by the tiny pesticide droplets—often less than one ounce per acre is used—everyone interviewed agreed that the most important component of mosquito con-trol is addressing the pests before they take to the air as adults. That means applying larvacides to mosquito breeding grounds, including standing water. It also means educating residents on how to eliminate standing water and of the importance of personal protection such as bug sprays and clothing that fully covers the skin.

"I'm not terribly in favor of spraying, but during times when people are getting sick and dying, we have to take action," said Apperson. "When you have a disease outbreak, the quickest way to bring down and stop transmission is by aerial spraying."

DDT Is Still Needed to Fight Malaria

Steffen Henne

Steffen Henne is a researcher for the Center for Industrial Progress, a for-profit think tank that promotes technological solutions to agricultural and other world problems.

Think for a moment about the last time you had a bad case of the flu: the headaches, the chills, the vomiting, the congestion, the depressed mood, the inability to function normally for days. But imagine it felt 10 times worse, and lasted for months or years, robbing you of anything resembling a truly human life.

That is life for the hundreds of millions of people who live with—and often die from—malaria.

The malaria parasite is one of nature's cruelest torturers. Acquired from the bite of the common Anopheles mosquito, this parasite enters the bloodstream and, left to its own devices, wreaks havoc on the lives of its human hosts.

In its milder forms, the malaria parasite leads to cycles of different symptoms including fever, sweat and chills, muscle pains, shock, and breathing problems. More dangerous variants lead to liver failure, coma, and brain damage. And, of course, there are the deaths—millions and millions of individual lives ended prematurely, usually after enough suffering to make death a relief. The most common malaria deaths afflict the most vulnerable—children under 5, pregnant women, and individuals who are already weakened by malnutrition or other diseases.

When you hear of "living in harmony" with nature, remember this: nature gives us unmitigated malaria, while human ingenuity and industry gave us the ultimate weapon against malaria—the industrial, "artificial" chemical DDT. As the National Academy of Sciences said in the 1970s, "[T]o only a few chemicals does man owe as great a debt as to DDT ... in little more than two decades, DDT has prevented 500 million human deaths, due to malaria, that otherwise would have been inevitable."

The Discovery of DDT

In 1939, Paul Müller discovered that Dichloro-Diphenyl-Trichloroethane, or DDT, is an effective chemical agent against insects such as flies, mosquitoes, and beetles. Science Heroes.com gives a good account of the story.

Müller was an independent scientist often referred to in the labs as a lone wolf. . . . Two events occurred that influenced his research into insecticides. The first was a severe food shortage in Switzerland, which demonstrated the need for better insect control of crops. The second event was the Russian typhus epidemic, the largest typhus epidemic in history. Müller, with his background in chemistry and botany, found himself both motivated and prepared for the challenge.

Because DDT was the result of industrial engineering and scientific selection aimed specifically at fighting bugs and benefiting humans, it provided a new level of effectiveness and safety.

He worked for J.R. Geigy (which eventually became today's drug giant Novartis), developing tanning methods for protecting clothes from insects, and a safe seed disinfectant that wasn't based on poisonous mercury compounds, as was common in his era. After these successes, he decided to pursue the perfect synthetic insecticide. He absorbed all the information possible on the subject, came up with properties such an insecticide would exhibit, and set forth on his solitary quest to find it. After four years of work and 349 failures, in September of 1939, Müller placed a compound in his fly cage. After a short while the flies dropped and died. What he had found was DDT.

Others quickly used Müller's work, which went on to win the Nobel Prize in Medicine, to combat insect-borne diseases. In one success story, 1.3 million people were treated with DDT to defeat a typhus epidemic in Naples during the winter of 1943/44 that no other treatment could stop. The DDT killed the lice that carried the disease, stopping the epidemic at its root. So began an epic war against nature's deadliest insects.

The DDT Revolution

DDT was a revolution in both effectiveness and safety. Prior to DDT and other modern pest control agents, pesticides typically included poisons such as arsenic or cyanide, which often did more harm than good. Because DDT was the result of industrial engineering and scientific selection aimed specifically at fighting bugs and benefiting humans, it provided a new level of effectiveness and safety. It could kill bugs but be eaten safely by humans.

By the 1960s, thanks to widespread deployment of DDT, malaria was essentially eradicated in the developed world.

DDT has numerous qualities desirable in an insecticide. It is a white, almost odorless powder that does not easily break down, even over long periods of time and is only slightly soluble in water. Once DDT was deployed in a given area, it could win enduring victories over deadly insects. Thus, it was used amply; direct deployment on the human body, spraying of parasite-infested areas, inside homes, mosquito-breeding waters, and large-scale deployment over crop fields were commonplace in the early years of use in the US.

Today great efforts are made to find a viable vaccine against malaria and to improve medical treatments for those who have contracted it. But the disease is not an easy target. There are many strains of the parasite and several variants of the Anopheles mosquito can serve as a carrier. Due to the short life-cycles of mosquitoes the malaria parasite can spread rapidly. Fortunately, DDT continues to prove reliable 70 years after its introduction, possessing a mixture of qualities unmatched by alternatives. Its longevity minimizes repeat treatments, further increasing reliability as well as affordability. Its safety for humans and animals makes it usable inside homes and close to potential malaria victims. And DDT has multiple ways of stopping deadly insects; even those that develop a resistance to its poison are still repelled by it.

The Success of DDT Against Malaria

The historical record is definitive on all these counts. In the decades following Müller's discovery, DDT proved highly versatile at defeating insect-borne diseases. By the 1960s, thanks to widespread deployment of DDT, malaria was essentially eradicated in the developed world. Acquiring malaria in the Western world today is unthinkable, but in the 1930s it was commonplace. Malaria had been widespread even in industrialized countries, where it killed thousands every year and infected many more. The popular misconception that malaria is only a tropical disease is only plausible because DDT eradicated malaria from northern latitudes within a generation. And DDT's beneficent impact went far beyond malaria. It has proved effective against many other insect-borne diseases, such as yellow fever and typhus.

Poor countries also benefited greatly from DDT. In Sri Lanka, malaria declined from 2.8 million cases and thousands of deaths in 1948 to fewer than 30 cases and zero deaths in

1964. In India the annual death toll declined from many hundreds of thousands in 1935 to about 1,500 in 1975.

The list of success stories in developing countries is lengthy. With few exceptions, DDT proves effective wherever it is used, and malaria cases spike where its use is discontinued. A more recent example is South Africa, where DDT was successfully used for malaria control from 1946 to 1996. After switching to another insecticide the cases increased 80-fold. In 2000 DDT was reintroduced and demonstrated its effectiveness once more, reducing cases significantly from a peak in 2000–2001 of more than 60000 cases and more than 400 deaths to less than 6000 cases and only 37 deaths in 2007. The alternative pesticide—synthetic pyrethroids—was unable to match DDT's results.

Although none of [Rachel] Carson's claims could withstand scrutiny, not even those about birds, the damage in public opinion was catastrophic.

The Campaign Against DDT

Unfortunately, despite the heroically positive impact of DDT, the modern environmentalist movement made this agent of life its number one target in the 1960s. In her famous book *Silent Spring* the environmentalist icon Rachel Carson chose, of all the features of industrial capitalism, DDT to demonize. Evading its benefits for billions, she made allegations about detrimental effects of DDT and other pesticides on human health and that of various other species (especially birds), based on junk science and anecdotes.

Revealingly, an intellectual and media establishment bred with anti-industrial hostility accepted Carson's narrative. Blinded to the good of DDT and eager to seize on Carson's bizarre characterization, they made her a cultural hero, which she remains today.

Although none of Carson's claims could withstand scrutiny, not even those about birds, the damage in public opinion was catastrophic. In the late 1960s and early 1970s, environmentalist and conservationist groups such as the Audubon Society and the Sierra Club spearheaded a call for a DDT ban.

In 1972, after 7 months of investigation of DDT by the newly founded Environmental Protection Agency (EPA), EPA administrative law judge Edmund Sweeney ruled against a ban. He found, based on the science presented, that "DDT is not a carcinogenic hazard to man," "DDT is not a mutagenic or teratogenic hazard to man," "The use of DDT under the regulations involved here do not have a deleterious effect on freshwater fish, estuarine organisms, wild birds or other wildlife," and that "The evidence in this proceeding supports the conclusion that there is a present need for the essential uses of DDT."

But EPA head William Ruckelshaus overruled Sweeney and banned DDT for general use, stating that "the long-range risk of continued use of DDT ... is unacceptable and outweighs any benefits," a statement based on blind anti-industrial ideology defying scientific evidence and decades of experience with widespread DDT use in the US and elsewhere.

The absence of facts behind the attacks on DDT indicates that environmenalists attack it not out of a concern for human safety, but on an ideological hatred of industrial chemicals.

Ruckelshaus never attended the 7 month investigation's hearings. But he did apparently read *Silent Spring*; in his opinion and order he credited Rachel Carson's book for raising awareness of the widespread use of DDT and other pesticides.

This marked a major political victory for the environmentalist movement. Although the case against DDT was not based on observable facts and sound science, the greens had acquired political influence.

Ironically, DDT's success made it easier to demonize. As malaria and other diseases vanished from the industrialized world, the need for DDT was not as immediately perceivable. Western populations became more susceptible to scare stories about industrial chemicals, while oblivious to those chemicals' life-saving benefits.

One example was the claim—often repeated today—that birds of prey, in particular the Bald Eagle, suffered from egg-shell thinning and other effects of DDT, allegedly bringing them to the brink of extinction. As it turns out, the Bald Eagle had been threatened with extinction at least since the early 1920s, more than 20 years before the first deployment of DDT, and increased in numbers during peak years of US DDT deployment. The connection between eggshell thinning or other detrimental effects and DDT could not be established by following scientific investigations.

Another common environmentalist critique of DDT is that insects develop resistance to it. (This claim was made by Greenpeace's Ryan Rittenhouse in a recent debate with CIP's Alex Epstein.) While resistance is a real problem with all chemicals used for controlling insect-borne diseases, DDT again proves superior to alternatives. In addition to its poisoning effect DDT also works as a repellent even if the insects have acquired resistance to it.

Even if these allegations were true they would not justify banning a pesticide with DDT's track record of enormous benefits. The absence of facts behind the attacks on DDT indicates that environmenalists attack it not out of a concern for human safety, but on an ideological hatred of industrial chemicals.

Parallel to the propaganda efforts to demonize DDT as a dangerous and highly toxic substance, aid organizations and governments applied pressure to halt third-world countries from using DDT to save their citizens. A recent example is

Uganda where in 2004 the EU threatened "dire consequences" for the country's exports if the western anti-DDT standards weren't met.

Influenced by donor agencies like the United States Agency for International Development (USAID), international bodies like the United Nations Environment Programme (UNEP), and other organizations, countries that depended on the aid were inclined to stop using DDT or not introducing it for disease-control. Belize and Bolivia, among others, have dropped the use of DDT out of fear of losing foreign subsidies.

Declining worldwide use of DDT also resulted in less availability for poor countries. India is the only country left producing DDT in large amounts. To combat this problem 15 African countries recently declared they would start producing the chemical for use against malaria mosquitoes.

Instead of encouraging the proven and effective DDT, a concerted effort was made to promote alternatives such as insecticide-impregnated bed nets and vaccines. The results failed to reach the promised levels. Subsequently, the World Health Organization (WHO), thanks to the influence of anti-malaria advocates on public opinion, changed its guidelines to encourage a more widespread use of DDT, acknowledging the unreasonable fear of environmental and health impacts. According to their own press release that constituted a "reversing" of their policy.

The result of [the] ideology-driven campaign against the use of DDT is a re-emergence of malaria in places where it was believed to be under control.

In 2001 at the Stockholm Convention to ban persistent organic pollutants (POPs), also named the "dirty dozen" and including DDT, environmental organizations demonstrated their opposition against DDT for any use. The World Wildlife Fund

(WWF), Greenpeace, UNEP, Physicians for Social Responsibility, and many others advocated against an exemption allowing DDT use for human health. Thanks to resistance of developing countries and anti-malaria advocates they had to back down.

Despite recent efforts of environmental groups to re-write their history on DDT, the record is clear. Their advocacy against DDT was never based on facts and sound science but on their anti-industrial, ultimately anti-human ideology. Their stated goal was and continues to be to get rid of this marvellous chemical because it constitutes a fundamental modification of nature by man, not because it does actual harm that outweighs the benefits of its use.

A New Malaria Threat

The result of this ideology-driven campaign against the use of DDT is a re-emergence of malaria in places where it was believed to be under control and the continuing high death toll in places where it was not effectively used yet, namely sub-Saharan Africa, parts of South America and Asia.

At its peak malaria infected hundreds of millions of people and killed over one million every year during the past decades. Today it is estimated that still about 650,000 human beings die every year from it. Many of these victims could likely have been avoided had the campaign against DDT not taken place and the success story of this pesticide been allowed to continue and spread into the poorer regions of the world.

The only way to stop the carnage is to embrace DDT, and industrial progress more broadly, as agents of human prosperity and happiness.

Greener Methods Are More Successful Against Malaria than DDT

Sonia Shah

Sonia Shah is a science journalist whose writing has appeared in various magazines as well as online. She also is the author of The Fever: How Malaria Ruled Humankind for 500,000 Years, *published in 2010.*

For over half a century, the battle against malaria has been waged with powerful anti-malarial drugs and potent mosquito-killing insecticides, weapons born from the wonders of synthetic chemistry. In recent years, however, fed up with the financial and ecological drawbacks of chemical warfare, malarious communities from China to Tanzania to Mexico have been forging a new way to fight the scourge, one that draws inspiration from the lessons of ecology more than chemistry. Rather than attempt to destroy mosquitoes and parasites outright, these new methods call for subtle manipulations of human habitats and the draining of local water bodies—from puddles to irrigation canals—where malarial mosquitoes hatch.

Green Methods in Mexico and China

The most striking example comes from Mexico, which has completely abandoned its previously lavish use of DDT [a chemical insecticide] in malaria control for insecticide-free methods and has seen malaria cases plummet.

Like many countries, Mexico for decades relied upon insecticides to fight the disease, by spraying mosquito-killing

Sonia Shah, "Turning to Greener Weapons in the Battle Against Malaria," *Yale Environment 360*, May 3, 2010. e360.yale.edu. Copyright © 2010 by Sonia Shah. All rights reserved. Republished with permission.

chemicals on the interior walls of homes where blood-feeding mosquitoes rest, among other methods. Between 1957 and 1999, taming Mexico's malaria required 70,000 tons of DDT.

New, environmentally-sensitive methods, such as clearing vegetation along waterways and around homes, were introduced in Oaxaca, the country's most malarious region, in 1998. By 2002, malaria cases had fallen from more than 17,500 to just 254, and Mexico incorporated the new methods into its national anti-malaria program. By 2000, Mexico had completely phased out use of DDT in malaria control; by 2002, it had phased out all other insecticides in malaria control as well, while simultaneously keeping malaria in check. No deaths from malaria were reported in Mexico in 2008, the most recent year of data available from the World Health Organization.

Similarly, in Sichuan, China, new, non-chemical methods involving the manipulation of water flow in irrigation canals have led to the near cessation of malaria, with malaria rates plummeting from 4 per 10,000 in 1993, to less than 1 per 10,000 by 2004. In several counties of the province, no malaria cases were reported at all between 2001 and 2004. Similar non-chemical gains against the disease have been achieved in Dar es Salaam, Tanzania, as well.

Anything that decreases mosquito longevity—a dearth of useful places to hide from predators, say, or excessively dry conditions—can also effectively squelch malaria.

Malaria currently infects 300 million people a year and kills nearly one million, and though the incidence of malaria is decreasing in some countries, it still rages in many others.

A Disease of the Environment

The new, greener methods of control rely upon insights into the exacting set of local environmental conditions that malaria transmission requires. While it is commonly considered a disease of poverty, malaria is just as much a disease of the environment. In part, that's because both malaria parasites and the mosquitoes that carry them thrive in warm, humid conditions.

But it is also because malaria-carrying mosquitoes, all of which hail from the genus *Anopheles*, don't generally venture far from where they hatch, and each species tends to lay its eggs in a specific kind of water body. Some prefer shady, flowing waters; others require sunlit puddles. Some can tolerate brackish water, while others must have clear water. That means that if people's exposure to the habitats of local malarial mosquitoes can be reduced, they will get fewer bites, and thus less malaria.

Malaria transmission is also critically dependent on the life span of the mosquito. The malaria parasite won't become infective inside the insect until it completes a 7–12 day cycle of development. That means that anything that decreases mosquito longevity—a dearth of useful places to hide from predators, say, or excessively dry conditions—can also effectively squelch malaria.

In Oaxaca, Mexico, malariologists found that the local malaria vector, *Anopheles pseudopunctipennis*, hatches from the still, algae-choked waters on the edges of streams, rarely flying more than 2 kilometers from its birthplace. And so, starting in 1999, they recruited volunteers in malarious communities to remove green algae and trash from the rivers and streams near their settlements.

"As a gift," says Jorge Mendez, former chief of Mexico's anti-malaria agency in the Ministry of Health, "we gave house paint to the local residents, to motivate community participation." The density of *Anopheles* larvae dropped by 90 percent within three years. Mexican health officials made life more dangerous for the surviving insects, too, by clearing the vegetation around domiciles, where *Anopheles* mosquitoes hid from both predators and the desiccating sunshine. They also provided prophylactic anti-malarial drugs. The program ultimately cost 75 percent less than the insecticide-reliant one it replaced.

In Sichuan, China, *Anopheles hyrcanus* prefers the standing water found in rice paddies, traditionally kept permanently flooded. A water-saving "wet/dry" irrigation scheme introduced in 1994 called for periodically drying out the rice fields. "The Chinese have fine-tuned this to an art," says Princeton University malariologist Burton Singer. The result was the destruction of *Anopheles'* larval habitats, a four-fold reduction in malaria, and increased harvests to boot.

Low-tech ... [anti-malaria] programs recall an earlier, pre-chemical era, when malaria control workers made similar gains against the disease by tinkering with the local environment.

In Dar es Salaam, Tanzania, *Anopheles gambiae* lays its eggs in trash-blocked sewer drains, and so community workers there began a program of clearing drains and spreading the microbial insecticide *Bacillus thuringiensis* into sewers. "This was the lowest-hanging fruit of them all," says Gerry Killeen of the Ifakara Health Institute in Tanzania, "the most basic and undramatic environmental management." It led to a 30 percent drop in *A. gambiae*'s transmission of malaria.

Other techniques, useful in areas where destroying or minimizing mosquito habitats is untenable, can be as simple as making sure people close the caves of their houses. More capital-intensive methods include leveling roads to avoid the formation of puddles, and installing running water and sanitation systems so that homes are less likely to be near stagnant water.

Environmental Management Methods More Sustainable

These nuanced—but decidedly low-tech—programs recall an earlier, pre-chemical era, when malaria control workers made similar gains against the disease by tinkering with the local environment, mostly because they had few other options. In the copper mines of Zambia during the 1930s, for example, malariologists significantly reduced malaria by clearing vegetation, removing obstructions from local waterways, and draining flooded areas. In Panama, during the building of the canal in the early 1900s, anti-malaria workers drained swamps and coated puddles with a thin skin of larvae-suffocating oil, part of a multi-pronged anti-malaria strategy that enabled the canal to be built. Similar measures helped eradicate malaria in the U.S. South.

As dramatically effective and universally applicable chemical methods may be, they cannot provide the long-lasting sustainability of environmental management methods.

Environmental management methods fell into disuse after World War II, with the development of a string of synthetic insecticides and drugs, led by DDT and chloroquine. Powerful and highly effective, modern insecticides and anti-malarial drugs can kill malaria mosquitoes and parasites quickly and cheaply, wherever they are used, regardless of local conditions. They can be implemented in even the most remote locales, with minimal infrastructure.

Managing the local ecosystem to minimize malaria vectors, in contrast, requires concerted effort from local communities, and expertise not just from health officials, but from ecologists, farmers, and engineers as well. It is labor-intensive. Ditches must be dug, drains cleared, vegetation removed. And what might be the perfect salve in one place could be the worst possible thing to do in another. "The details of what you need depend on the local ecological conditions," says Singer. "You can't mastermind it with a master plan." And while insecticide-spraying campaigns, drug distribution, and the doling out of insecticide-treated bednets can bring malaria mortality down rapidly, reaping the benefits of environmental tinkering takes years.

And so today, while the preferred chemicals have changed—instead of DDT and chloroquine common in the postwar era, the chemicals of choice are now primarily pyrethroid insecticides, impregnated in bednets, and anti-malarial drugs based on artemisinin, an extract from the sweet wormwood tree—the emphasis on chemical control has not.

The current war against malaria in sub-Saharan Africa, for which financing from governments and NGOs increased tenfold between 1998 and 2008, calls for 730 million bednets doused with insecticides, 172 million homes sprayed annually with insecticides, 228 million drug treatments for malaria patients, and 25 million preventive drug treatments for pregnant women, to be blanketed across Africa's malarial heartland, as the inter-agency Roll Back Malaria Partnership has outlined. Today, 11 countries are conducting formal campaigns to eradicate the disease, and malaria declines in the wake of chemical-based anti-malaria campaigns have been reported in Equatorial Guinea, Zanzibar, Sao Tome and Principe, Rwanda, and Ethiopia.

And yet, as dramatically effective and universally applicable chemical methods may be, they cannot provide the long-lasting sustainability of environmental management methods. None of the chemical methods of malaria control last longer than a handful of years. Insecticide-treated bednets must be replaced or re-treated every three to four years. Drugs must be continually administered. Interior walls must be re-sprayed with insecticide every six to 12 months.

With sustained funding and political commitment, insecticidal and pharmaceutical treatments for malaria could, in theory, go on indefinitely. The trouble is that in the meantime, the malaria parasite and the mosquitoes that carry it become increasingly adept at resisting the chemical onslaught. *Plasmodium* parasites that could circumvent the killing action of artemisinin drugs have already emerged in parts of Southeast Asia. By 2007, artemisinin drugs were failing in up to 30 percent of malaria cases in parts of Thailand and Cambodia, and by 2009, those drug-resistant parasites had spread deeper into southern Cambodia. Experts worry that it is only a matter of time before these drug-resistant malarias spread into the malarial heartland in sub-Saharan Africa.

Environmentalists and farmers worry that the increasing availability of DDT for malaria control could result in surreptitious diversion onto farms.

Similarly, malaria-carrying mosquitoes that can resist the pyrethroid insecticides commonly used to treat bednets were first reported in 1993, and have since turned up across sub-Saharan Africa. In a 2005 study in Cameroon, just as many kids using treated nets came down with malaria infections as those using untreated ones.

While DDT is still used in indoor spray campaigns against malaria, resistance to the chemical—and related insecticides—is widespread.

"Our enthusiastic programs are again going to founder in the swamp of biological resistance," warned malariologist William Jobin, on the scientific website MalariaWorld in April.

Fears of Toxicity

Finally, as the chemical war against malaria intensifies, so, too, do fears of toxicity. While the volume of DDT and other insecticides used in spray campaigns against malarial mosquitoes is miniscule compared to agricultural use, environmentalists and farmers worry that the increasing availability of DDT for malaria control could result in surreptitious diversion onto farms. Concerns simmer, too, about the understudied problem of disposal of the insecticide-treated bednets.

The environmental management programs in Mexico, China, and Tanzania all arose in the wake of just such concerns. Mexico's program, for example, was implemented after a 1996 agreement with the United States and Canada to phase out all uses of DDT. The irrigation program in Sichuan, China was implemented after the cost of running a 1986–1993 program of insecticide-treated bednet distribution became unmanageable. In Dar es Salam, the local malaria vectors had adapted to the widespread presence of bednets by biting outdoors instead.

The benefits of environmental management techniques—their longer-term sustainability, ability to harness community participation, and lower overall costs—may tip the balance in their favor in other fronts in the war on malaria, too. Health officials from Ecuador and Nicaragua, for example, have been flocking to Mexico to learn about their malaria program, Mendez says.

Many experts hope these techniques—still limited to just a handful of countries—will become more widespread, not to replace chemical methods entirely, but as complementary alternatives that will reduce the use of insecticides and drugs.

"Current methods are good at dramatic reductions, but the resilience and long-term sustainability are open questions," says Robert Bos, a senior scientist for the World Health Organization. Adds Mendez, "We need to put on the table a new model, in order to get an enduring control."

CHAPTER 3

Are Pesticides Needed in Agriculture for World Food Production?

Chapter Preface

Although humans have been farming for thousands of years, farming methods changed dramatically in the last few decades. After World War II, farmers in the United States and other developed countries began using synthetic chemical pesticides and fertilizer inputs invented during the war to boost crop yields. Other changes—such as eliminating manual labor with large farm machines, growing large amounts of one type of crop (monocropping), and generally employing factory-like economies of scale—also were embraced in order to raise production, reduce costs, and maximize profits. As profits soared, agribusiness corporations bought out many small family farmers, and it became harder and harder for small farmers to compete. Supporters of this new system of industrial agriculture have pointed to its dramatic yield increases and its success in feeding a hungry and growing world population. Critics, however, argue that industrial farming is unsustainable over the long term because it is destroying biodiversity and the natural environment, poisoning wildlife, and threatening human health.

US agriculture uses about 75 percent of all chemical pesticides sold in the United States, with the rest used by industry, government, and homeowners. Each year, according to the latest 2011 report from the US Environmental Protection Agency (EPA), American farmers introduce almost a billion pounds of toxic chemical pesticides into the environment and the food supply. Although the EPA found that pesticide use in agriculture is declining slightly (948 million pounds in 2000 and about 877 million pounds in 2007), certain types of pesticides believed to be highly toxic are on the upswing. One of these is glyphosate, an herbicide sold by the Monsanto Corporation under the name of Roundup that is increasingly suspected by some scientists of killing fish, birds, and soil organisms important to ecosystem balance; creating resistant superweeds; and causing genetic damage such as birth defects and infertility in animals and humans. According to the EPA, sales of glyphosate have more than doubled in the last decade, from 85–90 million pounds in 2001 to 180–185 million pounds in 2007.

This dependence on chemical pesticides, critics claim, sacrifices the environment and health for profits: farmers, many of them large corporate businesses, reap monetary rewards without having to pay for pollution of soil and water and other environmental damage that is a necessary cost of industrial agriculture. Farming uses massive amounts of fresh water and, according to the EPA, US agriculture is a cause of up to 75 percent of water pollution problems in the nation's rivers and streams. Soils are also increasingly becoming depleted, many farm experts say, requiring ever more chemical fertilizers and pesticides. Meanwhile, biologists are worried about catastrophic biodiversity collapse due to the die-offs of bees, bats, amphibians, and other creatures critical to crop pollination and natural insect control. And scientists say agriculture is a significant contributor to climate change because of its reliance on oil for running farm machines and transportation, and on petrochemicals to make pesticides. Many studies document links between pesticides and increased risks to human health, from allergies and autoimmune diseases to cancer and nervous system disorders. Such a system, critics argue, is not a sustainable model for the future and must be reformed.

The biggest benefit of industrial agriculture, touted by its supporters, is its ability to produce a large volume of food, which many agriculture experts say will be needed to feed the world as the population increases over coming decades. Proponents of industrial farming accurately note that chemical pesticides and fertilizers and other conventional farming techniques were responsible for a dramatic increase in world crop production in the years following World War II. Increasingly, however, scientists and policy experts are suggesting that much more sustainable farming practices could provide a viable path to both feed the hungry and repair and protect the environment. Small, decentralized farms, advocates say, could produce food for local markets without using so many resources or causing so much damage to the environment. Smaller farms that focused on sustainable agriculture methods, some studies have found, could produce high yields similar to those produced by industrial farms. Also, low-tech farms would be much easier to implement in less developed countries, where poverty and food scarcity are a real problem. And a system of smaller farms might be more resilient in the face of weather problems or other effects of climate change, experts theorize.

The difficulty of making such a huge change in agriculture policy, however, looms as a major obstacle in any effort to move toward more sustainable farming. In the United States, for example, the agriculture and pesticide industries and their lobbyists pose a major political hurdle, especially considering that the federal government itself has for many years promoted and subsidized industrial agriculture. The authors of the viewpoints contained in this chapter present opposing views on this question of whether pesticides are needed in agriculture to feed the world.

Pesticides Crucial to Food Production Future

Alan Stennett

Alan Stennett is a Lincolnshire, United Kingdom-based writer, broadcaster, and journalist who writes mostly about issues dealing with farming.

How important are pesticides in the food chain? That was the question addressed by farmers, food processors, academics and the agrochemical industry during a seminar at the Rothamsted Research Centre in Hertfordshire.

The use of pesticides and other crop protection products are essential if the quality and quantity of food production is to be maintained, according to speakers at the Pesticides and the Food Chain seminar at Rothamsted.

Keynote speaker Prof John Pickett said that a combination of what he called 'the malicious practices' of pressure groups and elements of the media, and the requirement to push residue levels down to very low figures, could result in many existing products being pushed out of the market. That would be a disaster for world food supply, he said.

"These groups tend to forget that we have to protect our crops against pests, diseases and weeds," he said. "We cannot possibly provide for our own needs in Europe and those of the world's growing population if we don't. We have to use something, and, at the moment, that has to be pesticides."

Prof Pickett noted that other control methods were being worked on but they would not be able to do the job effectively for some time, if ever, he said. This would mean that the public would need to be educated about the relative risks involved in crop protection products in order that they could assess the need for them.

"These are very small risks indeed, but I am sometimes afraid that the public will not accept them until they start to find empty supermarket shelves as world demand for food rises," he said.

Essex farmer Guy Smith said that many children's books and programmes painted a picture of farming as a dangerous, polluting industry, an image supported by organisations like the Soil Association with its constant repetition of a 'poison' message.

He urged the overall food industry to get together to set up a 'targeted and well funded' counter campaign to explain the reality of farming and food production to the public.

Peter Watson, of Dow AgroSciences said that pressure on the food chain to reduce pesticide use and residues was now felt all the way up to the consumer, whereas the industry had previously only needed to convince the farmer of the effectiveness of a product. He characterised the European consumer as being wealthier, healthier and better informed, with a distrust of government, science and industry, but open to media persuasion, with a nostalgic view of a countryside seen only as a recreational area.

Consumers in the UK, he added, saw price and sell-by date as the prime considerations when buying food. He acknowledged the need for standardisation of residue levels within the EU, but anticipated problems in the harmonisation process if it was not adequately funded.

David Penlington, co-ordinator of Unilever's Global Sustainable Agriculture Project, told the meeting that his group were working towards a reduction in pesticide use, both by setting protocols for the use of existing products and by working towards new non-chemical pest control methods.

Science Reporting on Organic Food Is Out to Lunch

Joshua Gilder

Joshua Gilder is a senior director at the White House Writers Group, Inc., a policy communications firm in Washington, DC. He was also a speechwriter to former president Ronald Reagan.

If the American people are largely uninformed on scientific issues, as the media so often complains, is it possible that one reason is the appallingly low level of science and health reporting in the media itself?

Science is supposed to be about asking questions. Scientists have theories and hypotheses, but they are not supposed to have agendas. They are supposed to be constantly challenging their assumptions by taking what they learn and asking themselves challenging questions about it.

The most outstanding characteristic of science and health reporters, however, sometimes seems to be their unwillingness to ask obvious follow up questions if the answers might disrupt the narrative of their preconceived storyline.

The examples are almost endless. But science reporting basically bottoms out when it comes to food and health, particularly the pesticides, herbicides, and other modern chemistries that allow modern agriculture to produce over 99 percent of everything we grow in this nation.

Endless articles and blogs preach the health benefits of eating organic food and the theoretical risks of the "chemicals" used in mainstream farming. But these reporters almost never ask the obvious question: how do organic farmers prevent their crops from being devastated by the same pests— insects, weeds, and fungi—that have bedeviled farmers since the invention of agriculture?

The answer is surprisingly simple: organic farmers do use pesticides. Lots of them.

It's probable that most of the food you bought during your latest trip to the health foods store was grown with pesticides. The only difference is that the pesticides used to grow foods labeled "organic" foods have been certified by the National Organic Safety Board.

As Alex Avery of the Hudson Institute explains in *The Truth About Organic Foods* some of these can be highly toxic. One heavily used copper compound, copper sulfate, has caused liver disease in farm workers and has been classified as highly toxic by the Environmental Protection Agency. It would have been banned in 2003, except that organic growers protested that there was no other way to protect their crops from fungal disease.

Other organic pesticides could be labeled "natural," but that hardly makes them safer. Pyrethrins, derived from the African chrysanthemum, are powerful nerve toxins. Rotenone, also extracted from plants, causes liver and kidney damage and Parkinson-like symptoms in rats. Another flower extract, Sabidilla can cause paralysis and death in high doses and kills honeybee.

Used correctly, all these organic pesticides are likely as safe as the thoroughly studied and tested pesticides that mainstream farmers use. The difference is that unlike modern pesticides, whose use is highly regulated and monitored, the U.S. government makes no attempt to record the volume of pesticides used by organic farmers. Worse, many organic farmers are forced to use pesticides in much higher volumes than mainstream farmers because these organic pesticides are much less effective than synthetic ones.

And the amount used is probably the most important fact that we need to know, as a basic principal of toxicology is that "the dose determines the poison." In other words, at low enough doses, most things are safe. At high enough doses, everything is poisonous, including water.

But this essential scientific fact is rarely mentioned in the scare stories that fill the press and TV. And of course, the antichemical activists have become masters of exploiting this blind spot.

Thus, when the radical Environmental Working Group published their "Dirty Dozen" list of produce with pesticide residues (all at levels measured in parts per billion that couldn't possibly have any deleterious health effects), CNN's Sanjay Gupta simply relayed the group's warning to avoid conventionally grown produce and buy organic instead, explaining that organic food is better because it is grown "using materials of plant or animal origin, instead of chemicals."

Of course, this last statement is neither true nor to the point. But such passes for science reporting these days. When some brave writer dares to point these facts out, the activists and media generally ignore the substance of their arguments and accuse them instead of being shills for industry. Ultimately, however, it's the facts that matter. And it's the facts, not needless scare stories, half-truths and untruths, that the health and science media should be reporting.

Myths About Pesticides

Pesticide Action Network North America

Pesticide Action Network North America (PANNA) is an advo-cacy organization that works to replace the use of hazardous pes-ticides with ecologically sound and socially responsible alterna-tives.

Myths about pesticides are a testimony to the power of advertising, marketing and lobbying. The big pesticide corporations, like big tobacco and the oil industry, have sys-tematically manufactured doubt about the science behind pes-ticides and fostered the myth that their products are essential to life as we know it—and harmless if "used as directed".

The recent book *Merchants of Doubt* calls it the "Tobacco Strategy"—orchestrated PR and legal campaigns to deny the evidence, often using rogue scientists to invent controversy around so-called "junk science" to deny everything from cancer-causing second-hand smoke to global warming to the hazards of DDT. Here are eight of the seemingly plausible myths we hear every day:

1. Pesticides are necessary to the feed the world

2. Pesticides aren't *that* dangerous

3. The dose makes the poison

4. The government is protecting us

5. GMOs reduce reliance on pesticides

6. We're weaning ourselves off of pesticides

7. Pesticides are the answer to global climate change

8. We need DDT to end malaria, combat bedbugs, etc.

Myth #1: Pesticides Are Necessary to the Feed the World

Reality: The most comprehensive analysis of world agriculture to date tells us that *what can feed the world—what feeds most of the world now, in fact—is smaller-scale agriculture that does not rely on pesticides.*

A large and growing body of peer-reviewed, scientific studies document that pesticides are harmful to human health.

More to the point, hunger in an age of plenty isn't a problem of production (or yields, as the pesticide industry claims), efficiency or even distribution. It is a matter of priorities. If we were serious about feeding people we wouldn't grow enough extra grains to feed 1/3 of the world's hungry and then pour them into gas tanks. Dow, Monsanto, Syngenta and other pesticide producers have marketed their products as necessary to feed the world. Yet as insecticide use increased in the U.S. by a factor of 10 in the 50 years following World War II, crop losses almost doubled. Corn is illustrative: in place of crop rotations, most acreage was planted year after year only with corn. Despite more than a 1000-fold increase in use of organophosphate insecticides, crop losses to insects rose from 3.5% to 12%.

Myth #2: Pesticides Aren't *That* Dangerous

Reality: Pesticides are dangerous by design. They are engineered to cause death. And harms to human health are very well documented, with children especially at risk. Just a few examples recently in the news:

- An entire class of pesticides (organophosphates) has been linked to higher rates of ADHD in children.

- The herbicide atrazine, found in 94% of our water supply, has been linked to birth defects, infertility and cancer.

- Women exposed to the pesticide endosulfan during pregnancy are more likely to have autistic children.

- Girls exposed to DDT before puberty are 5 times more likely to develop breast cancer.

A large and growing body of peer-reviewed, scientific studies document that pesticides are harmful to human health. The environmental harms of pesticides are also clear, from male frogs becoming females after exposure, to collapsing populations of bats and honeybees.

The cornerstone of pesticide regulation is a fundamentally flawed process of "risk assessment" that cannot begin to capture the realities of pesticide exposure and the health hazards they pose.

Myth #3: The Dose Makes the Poison

Reality: If one were exposed to an extremely small amount of one ingredient of a pesticide at a time, and it was a chemical of relatively low toxicity, it might pose little danger. That's unfortunately an unlikely scenario. First, pesticide products typically contain several potentially dangerous ingredients (including so called 'inerts' not listed on the table [not shown]). Second, we're all exposed to a cocktail of pesticides in our air, water, food and on the surfaces we touch, and combinations of chemicals can interact to be more toxic than any one of them acting alone. Third, many pesticides are endocrine disruptors—which if the timing is "right" can do lifechanging damage to the human body with extremely low doses that interfere with the delicate human hormone system. Finally, the research considered when reviewing a pesticide is funded and conducted by the corporations marketing the product, leading to distortion of findings.

Myth #4: The Government Is Protecting Us

Reality: Our regulatory system is not doing the job. More than 1 billion pounds of pesticides are applied every year on U.S. farms, forests, golf courses and lawns, farmworkers and rural communities suffer illness throughout the spray season and beyond, and infants around the world are born with a mixture of pesticides and other chemicals in their bodies. "The prevailing regulatory approach in the United States is reactionary rather than precautionary," concluded the President's Cancer Panel in May 2010, "instead of requiring industry . . . to prove their safety, the public bears the burden of proving that a given environmental exposure is harmful."

The cornerstone of pesticide regulation is a fundamentally flawed process of "risk assessment" that cannot begin to capture the realities of pesticide exposure and the health hazards they pose. EPA officials remain reliant on research data submitted by pesticide manufacturers, who do everything they can to drag out reviews of their products, often for decades. Lawsuits are pending to force EPA to follow the law and speed up review. But a better, common sense precautionary approach to protecting us would *assess alternatives* to highly hazardous pesticides rather than accepting public exposure to pesticides as a necessary evil. Such a shift will require fundamental federal policy reform.

Myth #5: GMOs Reduce Reliance on Pesticides

Reality: Genetically modified organism are driving pesticide use, and no surprise: the biggest GMO seed sellers are the pesticide companies themselves. The goal of introducing GMO seed is simple: increase corporate control of global agriculture.

More than 80% of GMO crops grown worldwide are designed to tolerate increased herbicide use, not reduce pesticide use.

Monsanto, the world leader in patented engineered seed, would have us believe that its GMOs increase yields, will reduce environmental impact and mitigate climate change, and that farmers use fewer pesticides when they plant the company's seeds. None of this is true. On average, Monsanto's biotech seeds reduce yield. In 2009, Monsanto admitted that its "Bollguard" GMO cotton attracted pink bollworm—the very pest it was designed to control—in areas of Gujarat, India's primary cotton-growing state. Introduced in 1996, Monsanto's Bollguard seeds—which include toxic traits from the soil bacterium Bacillus thuringiensis (Bt)—now account for half the cotton grown worldwide. In India, the productivity of Bt cotton has fallen while pesticide costs have risen almost 25%, contributing to the tragic epidemic of suicide by India's debt-ridden farmers.

Promises to end world hunger through drought-, heat- and salt-tolerant seeds and crops with enhanced nutrition have proven empty.

In 2009, 93% of U.S. GMO soybeans and 80% of GMO corn were grown from Monsanto's patented seeds. "RoundUp Ready" corn and soybeans were designed for use with Monsanto's weed killer, and mostly they feed animals and cars, not people. Now that weeds are rapidly becoming resistant to RoundUp, Dow and Monsanto are introducing GMO corn that includes tolerance of 2,4-D, a more dangerous herbicide related to Agent Orange used in Viet Nam.

Myth #6: We're Weaning Ourselves off of Pesticides

Reality: After 20 years of market stagnation, the pesticide industry entered a period of vigorous growth in 2004. The global pesticide market is approximately $40 billion, and expected to grow at almost 3% per year, reaching $52 billion by 2014. About 80% of the market is for agricultural uses, but non-agricultural sales and profit margins are growing faster, driven by the rise of a global middleclass adopting chemically reliant lawns and landscapes. In addition, the industry strategy of promoting GMO seeds, most of which are engineered to tolerate higher applications of herbicides, has driven increased sales of weed killers.

Myth #7: Pesticides Are the Answer to Global Climate Change

Reality: Multinational corporations are working hard to increase market share by exploiting climate change as a sales opportunity. As of 2008, Monsanto, Syngenta, Bayer, DuPont, BASF and others had filed 532 patents for "climate-related genes," touting the imminent arrival of a new generation of seeds engineered to withstand heat and drought. Their approach will further restrict the age-old practice of farmers saving seeds with desirable traits—a practice that may prove even more important as the climate changes in unpredictable ways and demands more, not less, farm-scale diversity. In fact, evidence is showing that sustainable farming provides important solutions to climate change, with systems that create far fewer greenhouse gases, promote on-farm biodiversity and create carbon sinks to offset warming. Despite this latest gene-grab, none of these companies has yet been able to engineer any kind of yield-increasing or "climate-ready" seeds. Their promises to end world hunger through drought-, heat- and salt-tolerant seeds and crops with enhanced nutrition have proven empty.

Myth #8: We Need DDT to End Malaria, Combat Bedbugs, Etc.

Reality: The recent resurgence of bedbugs has nothing to do with the 1972 ban of DDT. Bedbugs, like many mosquitos, are resistant to DDT—and they were decades ago when DDT was still in use. In some cases DDT even makes bedbug infestations worse, since instead of killing them it just irritates them, making them more active. DDT had been abandoned as a solution to malaria in the U.S. long before it was banned for agriculture use, and around the world practitioners on the ground battling the deadly disease report that DDT is less effective in controlling malaria than many other tools. A small cadre of advocates continue to aggressively promote widespread use of DDT to combat malaria, bedbugs—even West Nile Virus—despite it's lack of effectiveness and growing evidence of human health harms, even at low levels of exposure.

French Scientists: 30 Per Cent Pesticide Reduction Possible Without Affecting Yields

Ben Wright

Ben Wright is a contributor to Farming Online, a website based in Europe that features news about commercial farming.

France is currently leading attempts in Europe to scale-back agricultural chemical use, attempting to halve the amount of chemical inputs used in the country by 2018. However, French farmers have reacted strongly to the targets, which they claim will affect their production.

The government has recently reintroduced several forms of green manuring and organic inputs for use on commercial operations in a bid to appease its farmers. However, although returns for France's farmers have increased and the government has received praise for showing commitment to the long-term viability of its agriculture industry, many farmers have become jaded by new environmental regulations.

France is currently being taken to court by the European Commission over its failure to designate adequate Nitrate Vulnerable Zones under a 1991 law. This has resulted in documented examples of water pollution as a result of chemical use, the Commission has claimed. France is currently Europe's largest consumer of pesticides, and ranks third in the world.

Reduction in Pesticides

France's agriculture department, INRA, last week stated, "The damage caused to the environment and human health by pesticides is a subject of growing concern. For this reason, during the Environment Round Table [Grenelle de l'Environnement], France fixed an objective to significantly reduce the use of these agents."

To support the targets, scientists at two of INRA's research units have demonstrated, using modelling techniques, that the country can achieve a 30 per cent reduction in pesticide use on arable crops without impacting on either yields or farm income.

The scientists, who were looking at whether France's pledge to radically reduce its pesticide use is economically and agronomically feasible, looked at expert opinions and past experimental results to design a series of scenarios for cultivation practices that would more or less reduce the quantity of pesticides consumed.

Chemical inputs are amongst the most expensive raw materials [and] ... reducing their use may save farmers money.

Their five-level classification examined a range of methods from intensive agriculture (using the most pesticides) to organic farming which proscribes their application. Between these two extremes were three intermediate levels, the researchers described as sustainable farming (which seeks to reduce input use), low-pesticide farming (which combines chemical and non-chemical methods for crop protection) and integrated farming, which notably implements crop rotations that can reduce the risk of biological attack.

Based on their modelling, looking at the whole of the country, the researchers were able to show that by developing low-input agriculture, a 30 per cent reduction in pesticide use could be achieved without reducing productivity or the margins received by farmers. However, a 50 per cent reduction in pesticide use, as demanded by the French government, caused only a 5 to 10 per cent reduction in yield at a national level.

Although the drastic reduction in pesticide use was shown to affect yields, such chemical inputs are amongst the most expensive raw materials, the rise of which has sparked concern across the European Union, reducing their use may save farmers money. The European Parliament recently commissioned a report into the rise in prices of agricultural inputs after concerns over the effect on farmers' margins. The INRA researchers concluded that, in order to attain France's goal of reducing chemical application, whilst maintaining food production, "A significant increase in the share of organic and integrated farming methods would be necessary."

Looking Forward

As a result of their study, the scientists suggested several measures for the French government to ease the country's transition to lower input farming. They suggested a system of grants and the taxation of pesticides which, if implemented in association with better delivery of advice and training, could convince farmers to reduce their use of these chemical inputs. There have been calls in Britain, since last year's National Ecosystem Assessment, for environmental impacts to be factored into policy and costs across a broad range of sectors.

In Europe, there have been increasing demands to increase research into more sustainable methods of growing. New Economics Foundation policy director Andrew Simms wrote this week of the pressures facing the world and the pressing need for more research into agroecological measures. He stated, "The technologies you choose matter, each carries with it a different DNA for the economy and society that surrounds it. The ones you pick can lock in a way of being for decades. We need to choose technologies for which low carbon and lots of jobs are part of that DNA. Step forward both multiscale renewable energy technologies and agro-ecological farming. As Jared Diamond put it in his book *Collapse*, societies choose to fail or survive. We are more aware now of the likely consequences of our choices than any society in history. Wouldn't it be embarrassing if we continued to make the wrong ones?"

An INRA spokesperson elaborated on France's desire to move past pesticide use, "Although their effects are diffuse and difficult to quantify, pesticides contaminate water and air and can cause illness, particularly among the farmers who apply them." The spokesperson said the study "Has shown that a major reduction in the use of pesticides, fungicides and herbicides is a wholly realistic goal from an economic point of view."

Although reducing dependence on finite petrochemicals, which are having adverse effects on the environments on which we all rely, is highly commendable, the INRA researchers' findings demonstrate that there is a pressing need for more research into truly agroecological production methods.

Organic Agriculture Is the Only Way to Feed the World Sustainably

Greg Seaman

Greg Seaman is the founder of Eartheasy, *a website that promotes sustainable living.*

Just a few generations ago, in the 1930s, approximately 45% of Americans lived on farms. This demographic gradually but steadily declined as people migrated to urban centers, and over time, to suburbs. Today, only about 960,000 people claim farming as their principal occupation, which represents less than 1% of the US population.

During the same period of time the US population has more than doubled, and demand for agricultural products has increased accordingly.

It is a testament to human ingenuity that the mechanics of farming has managed to keep pace with an ever-expanding demand even as the number of farms has declined. Farm machinery has become larger, more efficient and more productive. New crop varieties have been developed which resist common pests and diseases while producing larger yields. Chemical fertilizers and pesticides have become increasingly effective, allowing farmers to produce larger crops without the need for additional human labor.

But while today's large scale food producers continue to profit and consumers see supermarket shelves overflowing with farm products, the unseen costs of our dependence on agribusiness exert a mounting toll. Farmlands have become increasingly dependent on chemical fertilizers which have short-term benefits but contribute to soil depletion over time. Water retention is diminished in non-organic farmland, resulting in erosion of topsoil with chemical residues entering watersheds. We consumers have quietly accepted these changes in farming practices as the cost of feeding a growing nation, and because there seem to be no practical alternatives.

Recent experiments in small organic farming practices, and the release of a 30-year side-by-side farming study by the Rodale Institute, have shown this reasoning to be fundamentally flawed. Organic farming, both large and small scale, is more productive than 'conventional' chemical-dependent farming. Organic farming is not only the best way to feed the world—it is the only way to feed the world in a sustainable way.

Lower input costs for organic farm systems are credited with significant cost savings for the farmer.

Organic farms, contrary to conventional wisdom, outperform conventional farms in these ways:

1. Organic farms are more profitable than conventional farms

The bottom line for farmers, regardless of the practices used, is income. The 30-year side-by-side Rodale study showed that organic systems were almost three times as profitable as conventional systems. The average net return for the organic systems was $558/acre/year versus just $190/acre/year for the conventional systems. This figure is skewed because of the higher price organic farmers receive for their produce and meat, but the higher food costs alone cannot account for the difference in profitability. Lower input costs for organic farm systems are credited with significant cost savings for the farmer.

The relatively poor showing of GM [genetically modified] crops in the Rodale study echoed a study from the University of Minnesota that found farmers who cultivated GM varieties earned less money over a 14-year period than those who continued to grow non-GM crops.

2. Organic yields equal or surpass conventional and GM yields

The Rodale 30-year study found that after a three-year transition period, organic yields equalled conventional yields. Contrary to fears that there are insufficient quantities of organically acceptable fertilizers, the data suggest that leguminous cover crops could fix enough nitrogen to replace the amount of synthetic fertilizer currently in use.

In a review of 286 projects in 57 countries, farmers were found to have increased agricultural productivity by an average of 79%, by adopting "resource-conserving" or ecological agriculture.

3. Organic crops are more resilient than conventionally grown and GM crops

Organic corn yields were 31 per cent higher than conventional yields in years of drought. These drought yields are remarkable when compared to genetically modified (GM) "drought tolerant" varieties, which showed increases of only 6.7 per cent to 13.3 per cent over conventional (non-drought resistant) varieties.

Organic systems used 45% less energy overall than conventional systems.

The effects of climate change bring more uncertainty to farming, with increased drought predicted for some parts of the country. It has become obvious that weather patterns are changing, and looking to the future, food crops will need the resilience to adapt.

4. Organic farming is more efficient than conventional farming

Conventional agriculture requires large amounts of oil to produce, transport and apply fertilizers and pesticides. Nitrogen fertilizer is the single biggest energy cost for conventional farming, representing 41% of overall energy costs. Organic systems used 45% less energy overall than conventional systems. Production efficiency was 28% higher in the organic systems, with the conventional no-till system being the least efficient in terms of energy usage.

The extra energy required for fertilizer production and farm fuel use in conventional systems also contributes to greenhouse gas emissions (GHG). Conventional systems emit almost 40% more GHG per pound of crop production in comparison to the organic systems.

5. Organic farming builds healthier soil

While short-term benefits are realized with the use of chemical fertilizers and mechanized production methods, every gardener knows that soil health cannot be compromised in the long term. Eventually, soil-depleting practices take their toll as soil structure weakens, microbial life declines and erosion removes valuable topsoil from farmland.

The Rodale study found that overall soil health is maintained with conventional systems, but soil health is improved when using organic farming practices. Organic farming practices improve moisture retention which creates water 'stores' which plants can draw on during times of stress due to drought and high winds.

According to the Environmental Working Group and soil scientists at Iowa State University, America's "Corn Belt" is losing precious topsoil up to 12 times faster than government estimates.

6. Organic farming keeps toxic chemicals out of the environment

Conventional systems rely heavily on pesticides (herbicides, insecticides, fungicides) many of which are toxic to humans and animals. With more than 17,000 pesticide products (agricultural and non-agricultural) on the market today, the EPA [US Environmental Protection Agency] is unable to keep up with adequate safety testing. In fact, the EPA has required testing of less than 1% of chemicals in commerce today.

Many studies link low level exposure of pesticides to human health problems, and chemical residue from pesticides used in farming can be commonly found in air and water samples as well as in the food we eat.

Inactive ingredients in pesticide and herbicide formulations have been found to be as toxic as active ingredients, but are not tested for human health impacts.

We need to promote organic systems which respect the integrity of soil health and sustainable systems.

---

7. Organic farming creates more jobs

Industrial agriculture has replaced human hands with machines and chemical inputs. According to the EPA, in the last century agricultural labor efficiency increased from 27.5 acres/worker to 740 acres/worker. Joel Salatin, organic farmer and author of best-selling books on sustainable farming, views these statistics as another reason for us to return to our farming roots. "People say our system can't feed the world, but they're absolutely wrong," he says, "Yes, it will take more hands, but we've got plenty of them around."

One important aspect to consumer support of conventional farming practices is the cost of food. Organic produce and meat is higher priced than non-organic counterparts. But, according to Joel Salatin, we get what we pay for. "We spend around 10% of our income on food and some 16% on health care, and it used to be the reverse."

Our current food production system is in need of repair. We need to promote organic systems which respect the integrity of soil health and sustainable systems. Until recently it was thought that our national and global food needs were too big to be met with natural, organic food production systems. Recent studies confirm, however, that organic farming is the way of the future. We need, both collectively and as individuals, to support the organic food movement to enable the process to move forward with the research, seed development and farming practices needed to feed a hungry world.

CHAPTER 4

What Is the Future for Pesticides?

Chapter Preface

One of the questions that may affect the future of pesticides concerns the fate of genetically modified organisms (GMOs) and GMO crops—crops whose genetic material has been changed in order to improve agricultural yields and increase agricultural profits. GMOs burst into the news in the early 1990s as a way to quickly create beneficial traits in crop plants, such as drought resistance, higher nutritional values, and resistance to pesticides. Initially, many observers thought GMO crop technology might provide farmers with a way to use fewer pesticides and make crops better able to withstand droughts and more productive for feeding the world. In recent years, however, some evidence is emerging suggesting that GMO crops may not fulfill their early promise.

Many of the most well-known GMO crops were created by Monsanto Corporation, a large agricultural biotechnology company. Some of the first GMO crops produced by the company were Bt corn and Bt soybeans—crops that were genetically engineered to produce a natural type of bacterium called *Bacillus thuringiensis*, or Bt, which is poisonous to insect pests. Monsanto also successfully altered the DNA of crops such as corn, soybean, canola, cotton, sugar beets, and alfafa to make them resistant to glyphosate, a pesticide that is the active ingredient in an herbicide made by the company called Roundup. Monsanto promoted these so-called Roundup Ready crops, explaining that farmers could spray their fields with Roundup and kill only the weeds without harming their crops. Many promoters of this new GMO technology promised that it would reduce pesticide use. Millions of farmers tried this system, and today all commodity crops (such as corn, soybeans, canola, cotton, and alfalfa) grown in the United States are GMO crops.

Pesticide use did seem to drop at first with the planting of Bt corn and soybeans. Some scientists say, however, that farmers planting Roundup Ready crops have dramatically increased their use of the Roundup pesticide. One recent study found that pesticide use in commodity crops has increased 7 percent since the 1990s. Today, according to the US Environmental Protection Agency (EPA), 180 to 185 million pounds of glyphosate are used each year—a huge amount that represents almost half of all herbicides used in the United States. In addition, certain weeds (called superweeds) seem to be developing a resistance to Roundup, a phenomenon being reported in various parts of the country. Moreover, scientists are discovering that glyphosate may be harming soils and may be a threat to animal and human health. Glyphosate works against weeds because it is actually a chelating agent that binds to minerals and other elements, effectively starving plants of nutrients and causing them to die. This action, some scientists believe, removes vital nutrients from the soil over time, depleting the soil and making it less useful for crops as well as weeds. Other research suggests that glyphosate may be helping an organism to proliferate that causes animals who are fed GMO crops to experience reproductive problems—infertility, miscarriages, and spontaneous abortions. Some health experts worry that GMO foods could have similar or other health threats for humans as well.

If GMO crops are clearly implicated in negative effects on the environment and human health, this could have a significant impact on US agriculture. GMO crops are so widespread now that any fears about safety might seriously damage US agricultural exports. In addition, consumers would likely push to have GMO foods labeled in the marketplace—an action that US policy makers have so far resisted but which is common in Europe. GMO labels, industry representatives say, would cause consumers to avoid many products on grocery shelves and cause ripples of economic pain throughout the food industry. For now, however, pesticide and GMO seed companies are benefiting from record profits, and according to reporting by *The New York Times*, these biotech companies are resisting efforts to study safety issues. According to the newspaper, a group of scientists claimed in a formal protest to the EPA that the biotech companies are preventing access to their seeds, thereby preventing truly independent research from being conducted into the safety of GMOs. The issue of GMO safety is one of the pesticide concerns that may face farmers in the future. The authors of viewpoints in this chapter describe several other developments and issues that may affect the future of pesticide use.

The Government Must Protect Endangered Species from Pesticide Poisoning

Defenders of Wildlife

Defenders of Wildlife is a national conservation organization that works to conserve wildlife and habitat and safeguard biodiversity.

In the 1950s, the widespread use of environmentally pernicious pesticides such as DDT played a major role in the rapid decline of iconic species including the bald eagle, peregrine falcon and California condor. Though DDT was banned in the U.S. in 1972, other commonly used pesticides continue to do serious harm to endangered salmon, frogs, and sea turtles, and kill more than 67 million birds every year.

Under the Endangered Species Act, the Environmental Protection Agency (EPA) must consult with federal wildlife agencies to ensure that pesticide use does not unacceptably harm threatened or endangered wildlife. These consultations result in "biological opinions" based on the best available science that help EPA reduce the impacts of pesticide use on endangered wildlife.

EPA must continue to consult with the U.S. Fish and Wildlife Service and the National Marine Fisheries Service, and must be held responsible for following those recommendations. Making sure that EPA carries out its duties under the Endangered Species Act is critical to providing clean water, protecting imperiled wildlife and safeguarding human health.

Protecting Salmon in the Northwest

Pesticides harm salmon in many ways, including by killing them directly, affecting their food supply and habitat, impairing their ability to swim, and interfering with their ability to navigate back to their home streams to spawn. In addition to poisoning endangered fish, pesticides also pollute the water and land that humans depend on.

Under the Endangered Species Act, EPA must consult with the National Marine Fisheries Service (NMFS) on the effects of 37 pesticides on salmon and steelhead in the Pacific Northwest. NMFS has already determined that six of these pesticides are likely to seriously harm 27 protected salmon species. This includes three organophosphate pesticides that are also linked to behavioral problems in humans. One in particular, chlorpyrifos, is associated with delayed mental development and behavioral problems in children. Yet organophosphates have been found in every water basin sampled on the West Coast. In fact, more than 90 percent of waterways affected by waste from cities or agriculture contain two or more pesticides.

When adequately protected, healthy salmon populations and clean rivers create local jobs in fishing and ecotourism.

Of the 672 million birds exposed annually to pesticides on U.S. agricultural lands, at least 67 million are killed.

In 1988, before Northwest salmon populations had dropped sharply, salmon fishing provided income to more than 21,000 families and contributed more than $1.2 billion to the entire Northwest economy ($415 million to Washington state alone). A 2005 study also showed that restored salmon and steelhead fisheries could yield more than $544 million a year in economic activity in Idaho, with $196 million from direct, out-of-pocket expenses by anglers.

Protecting Birds, Bats and Pollinators

Excessive pesticide use is a serious threat to birds, bats, and pollinator insects that provide a healthy and productive environment.

Studies show that a single spraying of a highly toxic pesticide to a field can kill seven to 25 songbirds per acre, and many of these birds suffered from severely depressed neurological function after the spraying. Of the 672 million birds exposed annually to pesticides on U.S. agricultural lands, at least 67 million are killed. Because of a combination of factors, including habitat loss and chemical poisoning, over 50 pollinator species are now listed under the Endangered Species Act.

Consultations under the Endangered Species Act are critical to ensuring that pesticide use does not unacceptably harm imperiled birds, bats, and other wildlife that pollinate crops, control pests and limit the spread of disease.

At the national level, $14 billion worth of U.S. crops depend on pollinators, and the California almond industry relies entirely on honey bees to pollinate almond trees. Globally, some 87 out of the 115 leading global food crops depend on animal pollination including important cash crops such as cocoa and coffee.

Birds and bats provide tremendous benefits to humans by controlling insects and the diseases they carry. A single bat may consume up to 3,000 insects nightly, especially mosquitoes. In south-central Texas alone, bats were estimated to provide $741,000 per year of pest control services for cotton producers.

Birds provide similar services, and the potential consequences of their decline include the extinctions of plants that depend on birds for pollination and seed dispersal, increases in the numbers of insect pests, increases in crop damage, and the spread of human diseases via rotting animal carcasses.

Uphold ESA, Enforce Biological Opinions

Congress must uphold the scientific principles of the Endangered Species Act and reject attempts by the pesticide industry to undermine protections for imperiled wildlife that also provide clean water and safeguard human health.

Neither of these solutions requires "fixing" the Endangered Species Act, which is flexible enough to protect wildlife and human health while accommodating economic growth. By following the recommendations of expert biologists, EPA can prevent the unnecessary poisoning of endangered fish, birds, bats and insects and preserve the economic benefits that those animals provide.

Pesticide Industry Would Benefit from Farm Bill Provisions

Nancy Watzman

Nancy Watzman is an investigative journalist and researcher who works as a consultant to the Sunlight Foundation, a non-profit think tank based in Washington, DC, that seeks to make government transparent and accountable.

Tucked within the 1,234-page House farm bill expected to come up for debate next week are two controversial provisions benefitting the pesticide industry by reversing court-ordered federal agency policies designed to protect water and wildlife.

CropLife America, the major trade association advocating for agriculture chemical producers, such as Dupont and Monsanto, has pushed for these provisions, both the subject of extensive litigation. CropLife reported spending nearly $5 million on lobbying in 2011–2012, according to a search on Influence Explorer, as well as distributing nearly $250,000 in campaign contributions to members of Congress. Member companies are the source of millions more in campaign cash and lobbying clout. The group did not respond to an inquiry by the time of this posting.

One provision would permit farmers and others to spray pesticides on certain bodies of water without seeking a Clean Water Act permit first, reversing a 2009 court decision. It is based on legislation sponsored by Rep. Bob Gibbs, R-Ohio, and a member of the Agriculture Committee, who has collected $11,000 in campaign funds from agricultural services industry groups such as CropLife, Dow Chemical, and the Agricultural Retailers Association, according to a search on Influence Explorer.

In its 2012 annual report, CropLife notes that a previous version of the legislation passed the House in 2011, although it was not included in the Senate-passed farm bill last year. The group says it is "determined to put an end to this unnecessary regulation."

Another provision would prevent the Environmental Protection Agency (EPA) from restricting pesticide use near certain fisheries until there is a new study by the National Research Council (NRC) of the underlying science that informs the limitations. In its annual report, CropLife discussed working on amendments to "address the immediate threats posed" by the scientific evaluations, and referred its lobbying of the House on the matter as a "time out approach."

Industry groups argue that farmers should not be required to get Clean Water Act permits to spray pesticides on waterways because such chemicals are already regulated under the Federal Insecticide, Fungicide and Rodenticide Act.

In 2011, Zeke Grader, executive director of the Pacific Coast Federation of Fishermen's Association, which was a party to the original lawsuit, testified before Congress that pesticide restrictions are needed to maintain the health of local salmon. "EPA-regulated pesticides are now found nearly everywhere in west coast rivers and are killing salmon, destroying salmon jobs, and endangering public health," he said.

CropLife reported having a dozen lobbyists on staff and for hire in 2013. These include John H. Thorne, who has been lobbying on behalf of CropLife and several chemical companies on the issue of the Clean Water Act permitting for some time. Thorne prepared this PowerPoint presentation [not available] on the issue posted on CropLife's website, noting the issue would remain alive in 2013. While there is a companion Senate bill promoting industry's position sponsored by Sens. Mike Crapo, R-Idaho, and Kay Hagan, D-N.C., it was not included in the recently passed Senate version of the farm bill.

Industry groups argue that farmers should not be required to get Clean Water Act permits to spray pesticides on waterways because such chemicals are already regulated under the Federal Insecticide, Fungicide and Rodenticide Act (FIFRA). They say the 2009 court decision requiring such permits means "tremendous new burdens on thousands of small business, farms, communities, counties and state and federal agencies legally responsible for pest control."

Environmental groups have countered that FIFRA has not done an adequate job of protecting waterways, and claims the permitting process already contains exemptions for common agricultural practices. "EPA's general permit for use of pesticides applied directly to water is one step forward in safeguarding our ecosystems and communities from the larger problem of pesticide pollution."

While important to the industry groups involved, the pesticide provisions represent just a small portion of contentious issues that will drive debate when the House takes up the farm bill next week. Conservative lawmakers have vowed to slash the food stamp program beyond $20 billion already set in the bill. Another big ticket issue is crop insurance, which environmental and conservative organizations criticize as an expensive subsidy program for farmers. Heritage Action, associated with the conservative Heritage Foundation, has been running radio ads urging House members to oppose the bill. House Majority Leader John Boehner, R-Ohio, threw his support behind the bill today, despite his opposition to dairy support program.

Pesticide Use Is Increasing in Organic Farming

Jack Dini

Jack Dini is a columnist on environmental studies for Plating & Surface Finishing *and also writes for other publications.*

Pesticide use in California rose in 2010 after declining for four consecutive years. The data, released by the Department of Pesticide Regulation show an increase of nearly 10 percent in pounds used from 2009 to 2010. More than 173 million pounds were applied statewide, an increase of nearly 15 million pounds from the previous year.

Sulfur, a natural fungicide used by conventional and organic farmers to control mildew, was the most-used pesticide in the state. Its use grew by 10 percent and accounted for 27 percent of all reported pesticide use.

Organic Pesticides

Contrary to what most people believe, 'organic' does not automatically mean 'pesticide-free', or 'chemical-free.' In fact, under the laws of most states, organic farmers are allowed to use a wide variety of chemical sprays and powders on their crops, and sulfur is one of the most highly used 'organic pesticides.'

Data from the National Center for Food and Agricultural Policy in Washington, DC, show that two pesticides approved for use on organic crops are the most heavily used in the United States. Oil, an organic insecticide, was the single most used pesticide in 1997, with farmers using 102 million pounds on 22 different crops that range from almonds and walnuts to cotton and strawberries. Sulfur, an organic fungicide, was the second most used pesticide on US farms in 1997; growers used 78 million pounds of sulfur on 49 different crops, ranging from alfalfa and avocados to mint and watermelons. In fact, these two organic-approved pesticides alone accounted for over 23% of all US agricultural use in 1997, with oil accounting for 56% of all insecticides and sulfur accounting for 59% of all fungicides.

These statistics raise important questions. With organic farming still representing a small percentage of total US food production, what will happen to overall pesticide use if and when organic farming expands to supply a larger percentage of US food? How heavily are pesticides being used on organic farms in the United States? What are the environmental consequences, if any from the use of these and other organic pesticides? Are these greater or less than the environmental impacts from synthetic pesticides? Are there any potential human health risks from organic pesticide use?

[Researcher] Alex Avery reports on research that revealed one-fourth of all fruits and vegetables marketed as organic had significant residues of synthetic in them. Further, nearly a third of the time when the synthetic pesticides residues were found on organic produce, they were present at a concentration even higher than the average levels found on conventional fruits and vegetables. However, if you are an organic food proponent, before throwing your food into the garbage can, realize that this research has very little to do with real food safety. The traces of synthetic pesticides on both the conventional foods and the organic foods were well below safety levels set by the government. These standards use 100-fold safety margins. This type of research is mostly a testament to our technical prowess. One part per million (1 ppm), equivalent to one second in 11.8 days, was the analytical capability in the not too distant past. Today, one part per trillion (1 ppt), equivalent to 1 second in 32,000 years, and even better are possible. These days, researchers can find anything in any thing.

GMO Crops Are Resulting in Heavier Pesticide Use in Conventional Farming

Tom Philpott

Tom Philpott is the food and agriculture editor for Mother Jones, *a progressive magazine.*

For years, proponents of genetically modified [GMO] crops have hailed them as a critical tool for weaning farmers from reliance on toxic pesticides. On its website, the GMO-seed-and-agrichemical giant Monsanto makes the green case for its Roundup Ready crops, engineered to withstand the company's own blockbuster herbicide, Roundup:

> Roundup agricultural herbicides and other products are used to sustainably an [sic] effectively control weeds on the farm. Their use on Roundup Ready crops has allowed farmers to conserve fuel, reduce tillage and decrease the overall use of herbicides.

But in a just-released paper published in the peer-reviewed *Environmental Sciences Europe*, Chuck Benbrook, research professor at Washington State University's Center for Sustaining Agriculture and Natural Resources, shreds that claim. He found that Monsanto's Roundup Ready technology, which dominates corn, soy, and cotton farming, has called forth a veritable monsoon of herbicides, both in terms of higher application rates for Roundup, and, in recent years, growing use of other, more-toxic herbicides.

An Herbicide Gusher

Benbrook found that overall, GMO technology drove up herbicide use by 527 million pounds, or about 11 percent, between 1996 (when Roundup Ready crops first hit farm fields) and 2011. But it gets worse. For several years, the Roundup Ready trait actually did meet Monsanto's promise of decreasing overall herbicide use—herbicide use dropped by about 2 percent between 1996 and 1999, Benbrook told me in an interview. But then weeds started to develop resistance to Roundup, pushing farmers to apply higher per-acre rates. In 2002, farmers using Roundup Ready soybeans jacked up their Roundup application rates by 21 percent, triggering a 19 million pound overall increase in Roundup use.

Since then, an herbicide gusher has been uncorked. By 2011, farms using Roundup Ready seeds were using 24 percent more herbicide than non-GMO farms planting the same crops, Benbrook told me. What happened? By that time, "in all three crops [corn, soy, and cotton], resistant weeds had fully kicked in," Benbrook said, and farmers were responding both by ramping up use of Roundup and resorting to older, more toxic herbicides like 2,4-D.

GMO seed giants Monsanto and Dow are preparing to roll out seeds designed to resist both Roundup and older herbicides including 2,4-D, the less toxic half of the formulation that made up the infamous Vietnam War defoliant Agent Orange.

Problems with Bt Technology

Now, biotech industry defenders might counter that the surge in herbicide use is balanced by the other main product offered by the industry: seeds engineered to contain the toxic-to-insects gene found in Bacillus thuringiensis (Bt), a naturally occurring bacterial pesticide. The pitch is this: Rather having to spray corn and cotton with insecticides, plant our Bt seeds, and your insect problems are taken care of.

Benbrook found that the Bt trait indeed led to a reduction in insecticide use of 123 million pounds between 1996 and 2011. But that figure is dwarfed by the 527 million pound, GMO-driven increase in herbicide use over the same period. In other words, GMOs have added more than four pounds of herbicides to US farm fields for every pound of insecticide they've taken away. Overall, Benbrook found, GMOs have lead to a net increase in pesticide use (meaning herbicides plus insecticides) of 404 million pounds, a 7 percent gain.

And just as weeds developed resistance to year-after-year applications of Roundup, corn's number-one insect pest, the rootworm, is quickly evolving to be able to withstand Bt-engineered corn, as I've reported before. Benbrook told me that in areas of the Midwest where farmers have been planting Bt corn year after year—an increasingly popular practice, since the explosion in ethanol production that started in 2006—ag university extension experts are suggesting that farmers spray other insecticides to supplement the failing Bt trait in their corn. "The goal of this technology was to make it possible not have to spray these corn insecticides, and now we have to spray them again to bail out this technology," Benbrook told me.

A Continuing Chemical War

The chemical war against pests will likely get yet another boost from the failure of Roundup. As I've reported before, GMO seed giants Monsanto and Dow are preparing to roll out seeds designed to resist both Roundup and older herbicides including 2,4-D, the less toxic half of the formulation that made up the infamous Vietnam War defoliant Agent Orange. The industry insists that weeds won't develop resistance to the new products. But last year, a group of Penn State weed scientists published a paper warning that the new products are "likely to increase the severity of resistant weeds." Indeed, 2,4-D-resistant weeds have already been documented in Nebraska.

In his paper, Benbrook created a model for how a 2,4-D resistant corn product, if released in 2013, would affect 2,4-D use. One of the actual benefits of Roundup Ready technology is that it has until recently made 2,4-D almost obsolete—its use on corn crops went from 4.4 million pounds in 1995 to 2.4 million in 2000. It hovered at that level for a while before jumping to 3.3 million pounds in 2010, as farmers increasingly resorted to it to attack Roundup-resistant weeds. If 2,4-D resistant corn is widely adopted, Benbrook projects, making what he calls "conservative" assumptions, 2,4-D use will hit 103.4 million pounds on corn fields per year by 2019. Overall, Benbrook projects a 30-fold increase in 2,4-D applied between 2000 and 2019. Because 2,4-D is so toxic, the result will not be pretty. Here's Benbrook's study:

> Such a dramatic increase could pose heightened risk of birth defects and other reproductive problems, more severe impacts on aquatic ecosystems, and more frequent instances of off-target movement and damage to nearby crops and plants.

The only question on GMOs and pesticide use Benbrook's paper leaves open is: When will Monsanto correct the absurd claim on its website that its highly lucrative technology has allowed farmers to cut back on herbicides?

Biopesticides May Provide a Less Toxic Solution to Current Pesticide Problems

Sam Schrader

Sam Schrader is a frequent contributor to HealthWire, *a website that focuses on new developments in health-related topics.*

I don't think it's a secret as to how much I detest [biotechnology company] Monsanto and its inherently harmful products.

Unfortunately, most farmers cannot escape Monsanto's hegemony without using tons of potentially harmful insecticides. However, Marrone Bio Innovations (MBI) may have found a solution to that problem in the form of biopesticides.

The Biopesticide Solution

Biopesticides offer a number of benefits, including:

- Alternative modes of action to traditional products, which makes biopesticides an important part of most integrated pest management programs.

- Minimal impact on the environment and humans.

- Exempt from tolerances making applications flexible.

- High degree of worker safety.

- Can extend the life of traditional chemicals so fewer chemicals are used.

- Adds value to growers in both traditional and organic farms.

As of now MBI has four available products: Regalia, Grandevo, GreenMatch EX and Zequanox.

Regalia helps treat fungal and bacterial diseases in plants. It works by turning on the plant's own natural defense systems. When these systems are firing at full strength, a whole medley of fungal and bacterial diseases is almost rendered non-existent in a given crop. In fact, MBI's research states plants treated with Regalia produce and accumulate high levels of proteins that combat these maladies. Regalia can be used on almonds, blueberries, citrus, grapes, leafy greens, tomatoes, peppers and walnuts.

Grandevo is the first of broad-spectrum bacterial insecticide introduced in 60 years. This biopesticide contains an ingredient called Chromobacterium subtsugae, which can do away with insects that both suck and chew on the plant, such as stinkbugs and psyllids. Grandevo works by making the pest stop feeding on the plant and die shortly afterwards. In 2011, Grandevo was available as a liquid for citrus and vegetables in Florida, but this year it will be available as a dry formula to be available nationwide for all manner of crops.

Considering the hive collapse crisis of the honeybee having been linked to pesticides, non-invasive and environmentally conscious biopesticides are looking better and better all the time.

Weeding is one of the most time-consuming aspects of daily life on a farm. Trust me, I know firsthand having worked on one. MBI's new weed control biopesticide *GreenMatch EX* can help eliminate weeds. And its non-toxic and biodegradable. It controls most annual and perennial weeds. Its effectiveness stems from the active ingredient Lemongrass oil, which is very powerful. Lemongrass oil strips away the waxy cuticle of the weed's leaves, causing wilting, dehydration and eventually death. And unlike other oils, GreenMatch EX combines the Lemongrass oil with other oils that makes the effect last longer. GreenMatch EX can be applied virtually anywhere, even environmentally sensitive areas without wreaking havoc like other weed killing formulas.

Recently, MBI has branched out to creating biopesticides that work on aquatic pests. *Zequanox* is an environmentally compatible solution for controlling several different species of mussels. Zequanox is derived from a naturally occurring microbe that focuses its attack on zebra and quagga mussels without harming anything else. In fact, Zequanox is essentially composed of dead cells that, when ingested by the mussels break down their digestive tracts and kill them. Absolutely no harm is done to the surrounding environment and non-target species.

These four products are just the beginning. MBI is currently researching and developing an array of biopesticides that will hopefully render traditional pesticides extinct.

Considering the hive collapse crisis of the honeybee having been linked to pesticides, non-invasive and environmentally conscious biopesticides are looking better and better all the time.

Pesticides: EPA Is Pressed to Ban Chemicals That Studies Link to Honeybees' Demise

Jeremy P. Jacobs

Jeremy P. Jacobs is a reporter for Greenwire, *an online source for daily coverage of environmental and energy policy and markets.*

Where have all the bees gone?

The question has vexed farmers, beekeepers, regulators and scientists since the fall of 2006, when U.S. bee populations began their mysterious decline.

Approximately a third of U.S. bees have been dying in each of the last six winters, with a large percentage of deaths being linked to a phenomenon called Colony Collapse Disorder, in which entire populations of worker bees disappear.

Pesticides and Bee Decline

The cause of the decline remains unclear, but environmentalists—bolstered by several recent studies—have begun pointing fingers at pesticides. Several coalitions are now urging U.S. EPA [Environmental Protection Agency] to ban certain pesticides that are part of the widely used neonicotinoid family, even as the agency and pesticide manufacturer Bayer CropScience say the chemicals are safe.

Dave Hackenberg, a Lewisburg, Pa., beekeeper who was one of the first to spot the large die-offs, says regulators need to step in even if the science implicating pesticides is not conclusive.

"Something is going on," said Hackenberg, who signed a petition asking EPA to ban the pesticide clothianidin last month. "Maybe the pesticides aren't killing them dead. But at the same token, something is breaking down their immune system and something is causing all types of things to happen."

If bee decline is left unchecked, its impact could be substantial because bees increase crop yield and value. Experts estimate that the disorder has affected honeybees in 35 states and could cause $15 billion in losses to U.S. crop production annually, since roughly a third of the North American diet relies on animal pollinators.

Neonicotinoids were developed in the 1990s to replace organophosphate insecticides that were causing harm to humans. They are now widely used on many crops, including corn and soy, and in home gardening products.

Environmentalists charge that bees are harmed by neonicotinoids because they are absorbed by crops and present themselves in pollen and nectar, which are then foraged by bees.

Their concern is that the chemicals then affect the bees' nervous systems, and some recent research bears that out.

A recent study by the French National Institute for Agricultural Research in Avignon, France, that was published in *Science* exposed bees to thiamethoxam, another neonicotinoid, and tracked their movement. They found that the bees exposed to the pesticide were more likely to die away from their nest than those that weren't, suggesting that the bees' homing system was compromised.

"Our study raises important issues regarding pesticide authorization procedures," said Mickael Henry, the study's author. "So far, they mostly require manufacturers to ensure that doses encountered on the field do not kill bees, but they basically ignore the consequences of doses that do not kill them but may cause behavioral difficulties."

Other research from the United Kingdom that was also recently published in *Science* suggested that exposure to imidacloprid, a widely used neonicotinoid also made by Bayer, drastically reduced a bumblebee hive's ability to produce new queens. And those studies come on the heels of a controversial Harvard University study earlier this month that found even low exposures to imidacloprid also have significant effects on bees.

It's killing bees in massive numbers. We know that. We need to act now.

The studies have led to two petitions. The first, from a coalition of beekeepers and environmental groups, calls for EPA to ban clothianidin because, the petitioners claim, Bayer never proved it is safe in a field study.

Similarly, Susan Mariner, a Virginia Beach, Va., gardener, started a Change.org citizen petition recently calling on EPA to ban Bayer's products. So far, Mariner has picked up more than 136,000 signees.

"This is a factor in Colony Collapse Disorder," Mariner told *Greenwire*. "It's killing bees in massive numbers. We know that. We need to act now."

Use as Directed—Bayer

The controversy surrounding these pesticides, especially imidacloprid, is nothing new for Bayer.

It first flared up in the late 1990s in France after reported problems with a product called Gaucho. The company acted quickly, immediately conducting several studies and eventually pulling the product off the market.

David Fischer, a Bayer environmental toxicologist, said the studies proved several things. First, the chemical does pose high toxicity to bees, but only at levels around 20 parts per billion or more. Typically, he said, bees in the field are exposed to the chemical in a range of about 1 to 5 ppb.

It can also be hazardous when sprayed onto crops, but Fischer pointed out that the product's labels all say not to apply it when the crop is in bloom.

"We had a lot of independent university researchers working with," Fischer said. "And nothing that's come up in the intervening decade or so has changed that outlook."

When Gaucho was taken off the market, Fischer added, the health of the country's bees did not improve. He also pointed out that imidacloprid has been widely used in the United States since the mid-1990s, but the sharp decline in bees did not come until about a decade later.

Fischer's remarks were largely confirmed by the U.S. Department of Agriculture [USDA], which has done extensive research on the issue.

"What we've done, more than anything, is figure out what Colony Collapse Disorder is not," said Kim Kaplan, a USDA spokeswoman. "We have pretty much ruled out that it's any single cause."

Kaplan points to a series of other factors, including parasites such as the increasingly common varroa mites and tracheal mites as well as other diseases that may affect bees in the breeding process. Other factors may include loss of habitat or food sources, as well as diseases and fungi. In general, though, USDA has found that the larger the pathogen exposure, the worse off the bee hive is.

The agency has also questioned the methodologies behind some of the recent studies, including the levels of neonicotinoids to which the bees were exposed.

USDA's research is now trying to focus on two factors at a time and is currently researching whether exposure to imidacloprid and nosema, a disease, has a harmful effect.

Other experts suggest the answer may be even more complicated than that. Dennis vanEngelsdorp, a bee researcher at the University of Maryland, said there may be aspects of pesticides that are unexpectedly playing a role.

"There are a lot of suggestions that fungicides are playing a role and some inert components of pesticides, when they are mixed together, may have some toxicity," he said.

The [EPA] echoed USDA in saying that multiple causes appear to be contributing to the bee problems.

The scientist noted that traditional methods to combat diseases in hives are no longer working because they have developed a resistance. He also shot down the recent calls for bans on the pesticides.

"Just saying we are going to ban the product doesn't make a lot of sense to me because you need to have something that is going to replace it," he said. "It's implying that when you get rid of these chemicals, all our problems go away. I don't think that's the case. That's naive."

VanEngelsdorp did call for taking a closer look at how these pesticides are registered with regulatory agencies.

EPA said it is "concerned" about the issue. The agency has grouped all neonicotinoid pesticides together in its periodic registration review process and has moved up that review to this year [2012]. However, the agency echoed USDA in saying that multiple causes appear to be contributing to the bee problems. EPA also appeared to side with Bayer in saying that the pesticides are safe.

"Our review of these studies is underway," EPA said in a statement to *Greenwire*, "but at this time, we do not have data indicating EPA-registered pesticides, when used according to label directions, have caused Colony Collapse Disorder."

"Low-Cost Experiment"

That's not enough to satisfy Charles Benbrook of Boulder, Colo.'s Organic Center.

Benbrook has a simple way to resolve the issue: Ban the pesticides from some areas and watch what happens to the bees.

He bases the idea on stories he has heard coming out of Europe, where France, Germany, Italy and Slovenia have taken steps to suspend the use of certain neonicotinoids. In those areas, Benbrook said, bee populations appear to be on the rebound.

"If that is really true," Benbrook said, "we don't have to do a lot more science to determine what the logical policy response is."

Benbrook said that even if EPA did not think the science justified what he called a "moratorium," the agency could work out an agreement with certain states—like, say, Missouri and Arkansas—as a test case.

"It would be a very low-cost experiment," he said.

Benbrook pointed out, however, that EPA may face a legal hurdle if it tries to regulate the chemicals based on bee problems. Simply put, it is not EPA's job to prevent harm to bees, which it regards as personal property.

"Under EPA policy, they do not strive to minimize damage to personal property when they evaluate the label of a new use pesticide," Benbrook said. "So it's not really clear at all whether EPA has a statutory and regulatory leg to stand on."

John Kepner of the nonprofit Beyond Pesticides, which is also involved in one of the petitions, added that EPA's process for studying these effects is flawed.

"We know that there are these sub-lethal effects. They may be confusing the bees, causing fatigue or making it so they don't reproduce," he said. "But EPA doesn't have testing . . . for 'makes bees lazy.'"

He added that the honeybee problems could be providing insight to future problems.

"The honeybees," he said, "are definitely an indicator of what could be happening in the broader environment."

Are Pesticide Laws Strong Enough?

Angela Logomasini

Angela Logomasini is a senior fellow at the Competitive Enterprise Institute, where she conducts research and analysis on environmental regulatory issues. Safechemicalpolicy.org is a project of the Competitive Enterprise Institute, a public policy group that promotes free markets, limited government, and restrained regulation of pesticides.

There are lots of activist groups, green marketers, and others who claim that pesticides we use in our home, communities, and crops pose serious dangers. The underlying assumption is that existing pesticide regulations are insufficient to protect public health. Yet these sites never adequately explain the laws, the exposure levels they regulate, and likely health risks. The following overview of these issues demonstrates why consumers have little to fear from proper use of pesticides. Pesticide residues found on food, in gardens, and the environment in general pose little, if any, risk to public health, particularly compared with the enormous public health benefits of pesticide use.(1)

Unfortunately, the laws themselves may pose greater risks to public health because they are so absurdly stringent that they place in jeopardy the ability to address the greater risks associated with insects and other pests. Applying federal law, the U.S. Environmental Protection Agency (EPA) has banned numerous pesticides that are both safe and useful for farming, home pest control, and other public health purposes. The federal government regulates pesticides under three laws:

• Federal Food Drugs and Cosmetics Act (FFDCA). The FFDCA is the law under which the EPA sets tolerances for pesticides. The EPA can essentially ban a pesticide by not setting a tolerance—the amount of pesticide residue that is allowed to legally remain on food. The Agricultural Marketing Service, an agency of the U.S. Department of Agriculture (USDA), is responsible for monitoring residue levels in or on food. The U.S. Department of Health and Human Service's Food and Drug Administration uses this information to enforce tolerances on imported and domestically produced food in interstate commerce. The USDA's Food Safety Inspection Service enforces tolerances for meat, poultry, and some egg products.

• Federal Insecticide, Fungicide, and Rodenticide Act (FIFRA). To sell a pesticide, a company must also register it with the EPA under FIFRA. For pesticides used on food, the EPA can register uses only for pesticides that have a tolerance. Pesticide registrants must register and gain EPA approval of their products as well as for each specific use (i.e., use indoors as a bug spray requires one registration and use outdoors for a specific crop requires another). The EPA must review registered pesticides on a 15-year cycle. To gain registration, applicants must submit scientific data and research demonstrating that the products pose minimal risk. The EPA can limit uses by denying registration for such uses.

• Food Quality Protection Act (FQPA). The FQPA amended the first two laws in 1994. Details on these changes follow.

Brief History of Pesticide Regulation and Legislation

Before 1996, the FFDCA used two standards for setting tolerances. One standard allowed the EPA to regulate pesticide residues on raw produce using a cost-benefit approach. The agency could weigh the risks of using the pesticides versus the risks of not having them to help maintain the food supply. Under that legislative authority, the EPA applied what it called a "negligible risk" standard, allowing produce to contain pesticide residues that did not exceed a one-in-a-million cancer risk.

[The Food Quality Protection Act] applies a single standard for all pesticide uses and requires the EPA to show "reasonable certainty that no harm will result from aggregate exposure to the pesticide chemical residue, including all anticipated dietary exposures and all other exposures for which there is reliable information."

However, the FFDCA set a separate standard for pesticide residues found in processed food. It applied the "Delaney Clause," which prohibited the addition to food of any substance that caused cancer in laboratory animals. The Delaney Clause essentially set a zero-risk standard. It applied to pesticides used directly or indirectly in processed food. It also applied to pesticide residues found on raw agricultural products that were used in processed food, if the pesticide became more concentrated during processing. As science became able to detect increasingly lower levels of residues, the Delaney Clause essentially demanded that the EPA ban many pesticides. In addition, having separate standards for raw produce and processed food created perverse effects, which the National Research Council (NRC)(2) noted could actually reduce safety. In a 1987 report, *Regulating Pesticides in Food: The Delaney Paradox*, the NRC highlighted problems with the existing policy.(3) The NRC raised concerns about alternative pest control practices that could pose greater risks or could prove inadequate to maintain food supplies and control disease-carrying pests. The NRC called on Congress to address this issue, suggesting that it set a single standard for raw and processed foods.

In 1988, the EPA began applying the negligible risk standard to processed foods without legislative authorization. But in 1992, environmental groups succeeded in suing the agency for not applying the Delaney Clause. A federal court held that the agency was obligated to apply the Delaney Clause to processed food.(4) Hence, for those who used and produced pesticide products, reforming the law became an urgent matter. With numerous bans likely, many crops—and ultimately our food supply—would be placed in jeopardy. In addition, concerns mounted about the increasing difficulty associated with controlling rising infectious diseases, carried by insects and other pests.(5)

Meanwhile, environmental groups worked to make the law more stringent. Their efforts were bolstered by a 1993 NRC report and the media hype that followed. The report, *Pesticides in the Diets of Infants and Children*, noted that children might be more susceptible to pesticides and hence they faced greater risks.(6) Despite media hype suggesting the contrary, the study did not conclude that existing exposures were unsafe for children. Specifically, the study noted that "exposures occurring earlier in life can lead to greater or lower risk of chronic toxic effects such as cancer than exposures occurring later in life."(7) Just to be safe, the report recommended that EPA use a 10-fold safety.

Food Quality Protection Act Reforms

The FQPA attempts to address the conflicting standards within the first two pesticide laws. The FQPA changed the standard for setting tolerances. It applies a single standard for all pesticide uses and requires the EPA to show "reasonable certainty that no harm will result from aggregate exposure to the pesticide chemical residue, including all anticipated dietary exposures and all other exposures for which there is reliable information."(8) The FQPA mandated that the EPA apply this standard to all pesticide registrations, new and old.

Accordingly, the EPA is working to reregister the thousands of pesticides registered before the passage of the FQPA.

The [FQPA] law sets a general standard wherein the EPA must show "reasonable certainty" that a pesticide will "do no harm."

The bill was supported unanimously by both houses of Congress and lauded by members of agricultural states and farm interests. Many believed that it would dramatically improve pesticide approvals. But rather than solving these problems, the FQPA gave vital ground to those pushing for more stringent regulation. Not surprisingly, environmental groups supported the FQPA because they believed that it would prove even more stringent and would lead to many pesticide bans in the future.(9) Following the advice of *Pesticides in the Diets of Infants and Children*, the reform included several new criteria that now apply very strong standards to both processed and raw foods. When setting standards under the new law, the EPA must consider (a) the impacts of the pesticide on infants and children, applying a 10-fold safety factor unless information is available to demonstrate safety; (b) the aggregate exposure (the total exposure of individuals to various sources of the pesticide); and (c) whether the cumulative effects of a combination of pesticides could increase health risks.(10) In addition, the law created the Endocrine Disrupter Screening Program, under which the EPA must study pesticides that are potential endocrine disrupters.(11) The program is designed to simply add to the body of research on endocrine disrupters, but the agency has indicated that the program will serve as a guide for regulatory decisions.(12)

Food Quality Protection Act

In 1996, the Food Quality Protection Act (FQPA) amended the two federal laws governing pesticides: the Federal Insecticide, Fungicide, and Rodenticide Act (FIFRA) and the Federal Food, Drugs, and Cosmetics Act (FFDCA). Congress's goal was to address disparities between the two laws governing pesticide regulation and to address concerns that federal pesticide regulations were overly stringent. At the time, the onerous pesticide standards were leading the U.S. Environmental Protection Agency (EPA) to cancel many vital pesticide uses. The hope was that the FQPA would ensure a more scientifically sound process that kept risks low while allowing continued use of many important products. However, the FQPA created new and unexpected problems and may, in fact, prove as onerous as the former law. Although many have claimed that the problems emanate from poor EPA implementation, problems have also resulted from new onerous standards written into the FQPA. Addressing these issues will likely require congressional action.

Under the "cumulative exposure" standard, the EPA must consider the impact of groups of various pesticides.

Before entering commerce, pesticides must gain registration for each specific use (e.g., use as indoor bug spray or on a specific crop) under FIFRA. To gain registration, registrants must provide data that demonstrate that [the pesticide] does not pose an unreasonable safety risk. Without such EPA approval, firms may not sell any pesticidal product, although EPA can allow for emergency uses of certain products. In addition, the FFDCA requires that the EPA set "tolerance levels" for pesticides used on foods (as opposed to other uses, such as to control insects, rodents, or microbes). Tolerance levels specify how much pesticide exposure the EPA will allow as residue on foods. For example, the EPA sets a level that it believes, on average, will limit individuals' exposure to pesticide residues found on apples, assuming an individual eats a certain number of apples every day for 70 years.

The FQPA added some additional considerations. The law sets a general standard wherein the EPA must show "reasonable certainty" that a pesticide will "do no harm."(13) The requirement alone is quite stringent. The language and the legislative history indicate that this standard is equivalent to a risk not greater than one in a million.(14) But that is just the beginning. The standards must be even more stringent because under the FQPA, the EPA must now also consider the following:

- Aggregate exposure. The "aggregate exposure" standard requires the EPA to consider all exposure pathways of a single pesticide when setting tolerances. For example, the EPA must consider whether a person eating an apple that contains specific pesticide residue also is exposed to the same pesticide from consumer products, such as bug sprays or household disinfectants. Hence, the tolerance level for a pesticide would have to include all conceivable exposures—reducing the amount of allowable residue.

- Cumulative exposure. Under the "cumulative exposure" standard, the EPA must consider the impact of groups of various pesticides. There are two aspects in particular. First, it must group pesticides that supposedly cause cancer in a similar way—pesticides that have a so-called common mechanism for toxicity. Second, it must add all the exposures—inhalation, oral, dermal—of these pesticides and limit exposure to them as a group. This task is very difficult because the science is not always clear on the mechanisms for causing cancer for all of these substances, nor is it clear whether cumulative exposures actually increase risk. Claims about such cumu-

lative exposure risks gained steam with a study conducted by researchers at Tulane University. It claimed
that, when combined, endocrine disrupters were 1,000
times more potent. When other researchers could not
replicate this result, the Tulane researchers retracted the
study.(15) Despite the redaction, the idea that synergistic effects of chemicals multiply potency prevails among
activists. And the concept has even made its way into
law. After the Tulane study was published in *Science*,
Congress passed provisions in the 1996 FQPA calling
on the EPA to consider such cumulative exposures
when issuing regulations. Subsequently, several studies
reported no synergistic interactions with the chemicals.

- Safety Factor for Children. The new law requires the
  EPA to consider risks to children and to apply a 10-fold
  safety factor unless the EPA determines that a lower
  safety factor is acceptable. The EPA notes that it will
  apply this 10-fold factor in addition to the 100-fold
  safety factor it currently applies when setting standards.
  Hence, when the EPA applies the 10-fold safety factor
  for children, it will actually apply a 1,000-fold safety
  factor.

Already Conservative Risk Estimates Become More Stringent

Even before Congress made the law more stringent with the
FQPA, the EPA used very conservative risk estimates. Given
EPA risk assessment methodologies, pesticide safety regulations already applied safety margins that ensured exposure
levels were thousands of times lower than levels EPA deemed
safe. For example:

- Bureaucrats set standards to ensure safe exposures even
  if a farmer applied the full legal limit of all pesticides

licensed for use on a given crop. Yet farmers apply only a fraction of the legal limits and do not apply all pesticides licensed for a particular crop. For example, University of Texas Professor Frank Cross notes that one study shows that farmers in California use about 25 percent of their legal limit for tomatoes, and each farmer uses no more than 5 of 54 licensed pesticide products.(16)

- Cross highlights a number of studies showing that the EPA's conservative risk estimates overstate pesticide exposure by as much as 99,000 to 463,000 times actual exposure levels.(17) When researchers recalculated risks by considering actual pesticide exposure levels measured by the U.S. Department of Agriculture (USDA), they found that risks were "from 4,600 to 100,000 times lower than EPA estimates."(18) Applying the New Standards the combination of "reasonable certainty" of "no harm," "aggregate risk," "cumulative effects," and additional safety factors for children poses a host of new challenges for the EPA when conducting risk assessments for setting tolerances.

To assess aggregate exposure, the agency must estimate how much exposure the public has to a pesticide from the various pathways—on and in foods, in the home, and in drinking water. Then the agency must limit enough of those exposures to ensure that total exposure does not exceed the level it deems safe. To facilitate understanding of this process, the agency developed a theoretical construct called the "risk cup." The cup represents the total amount of exposure to the public of a pesticide that the EPA will allow. The EPA then registers only the amount of pesticide uses that "fill" the cup. When filling the cup, the EPA considers all potential exposure pathways. For example, regulators will estimate that certain agricultural use will fill 50 percent of the cup, drinking water exposure will fill 1 percent, home consumer products will fill 29 percent, and "other" exposures (which they assume but do not specify) will fill the rest.

Various groups have complained that the EPA has grossly exaggerated exposure levels. A key problem is that when the agency lacks data on actual exposures or when levels are below the agency's ability to detect them, regulators use default numbers that assume a certain amount of exposure. Hence, the cup fills, but it does not represent real risks to society. Once the cup is full, the EPA will not register any further uses of the pesticide.

When filling the cup, the EPA can consider the impacts of numerous pesticides—placing several in one cup. For example, the EPA has placed certain organophosphate products into one category and is working on a cumulative risk assessment for those products. Placing them all in one cup could demand dramatic reduction in registered uses. For example, home exterminators may not gain a registered use for many organophosphates, leaving them with fewer options for controlling pests such as cockroaches. Such changes can have serious public health impacts. In addition to carrying diseases, cockroaches are likely an important contributor to asthma, a serious health ailment affecting many children.(19)

"Minor Uses"

Ironically, a major problem relates to what people call "minor uses" of pesticides. Minor uses include key public health uses to control pests, ranging from disease-carrying mosquitoes to rodents. In addition, they include uses on many fruits and vegetables. These uses are anything but minor, yet the law has made many of them an unprofitable enterprise for a couple of reasons. First is cost. The law requires that firms spend a considerable amount of resources—submitting data and paying very hefty registration fees—to obtain a registration. Such high costs basically make many markets unprofitable for companies, so they do not bother to register those uses. The total cost of pesticide registration is estimated to be more than $50 million, and the process can take from 9 to 10 years.(20) Second, the FQPA standards limit the number of uses that the EPA will register for various products.

The Food Quality Protection Act could increase regulations on 46 percent of the uses of the 230 [organophosphates and carbonates pesticides]—a substantial increase.

These factors serve as disincentives for the development of new minor use pesticides as well as for the reregistration of old ones. In fact, to continue business in more profitable markets, firms are negotiating the elimination of minor uses when they reregister products. Syngenta, for example, came to an agreement with the EPA in June 2000 to eliminate many of the minor uses—particularly home-related pest control—for the pesticide diazinon. Syngenta explained that the product was safe when used properly. Agreeing to phase out certain uses was purely a "business decision," the company noted, because the product was no longer profitable for those uses.(21)

The FQPA's impact on minor uses promises to have serious public health outcomes because these products meet critical needs: to ensure affordable fruits and vegetables and to protect against disease-carrying pests. As one USDA official noted, even though the FQPA provisions were intended by Congress to ensure that existing public health pesticide uses are not lost without economically effective alternatives, the provisions may not be adequate. If the FQPA results in cancellation of major agricultural uses of a pesticide that is also used in public health, it may become no longer profitable for the manufacturer to produce small quantities for mosquito control, thus ending production of the pesticide. Since adulticides used for mosquito control were registered decades ago, the data supporting their registrations may be insufficient to meet current requirements.(22)

FQPA Impacts

The 1996 law has produced some serious impacts. For example, consider the effect of the law on products that use organophosphate pesticides. At the time the FQPA passed, there were 49 of these products on the market, representing about one-third of all pesticide sales.(23) The EPA picked this broad category of products in its first effort to implement the law's provisions on cumulative exposure. By the time the EPA released its draft cumulative risk assessment for these products in 2002, 14 products had already been canceled and 28 had to meet risk mitigation measures that include limitations on use, voluntary cancellations, cancellations of certain uses, and other restrictions.

Recently, EPA completed a 10-year study of 230 organophosphates and carbonates pesticides. It concluded that the Food Quality Protection Act demands that the agency ban 3,200 uses of pesticide products in these categories and places restrictions on 1,200 other uses. It deemed 5,237 uses as "safe" under the act.(24) Hence, the Food Quality Protection Act could increase regulations on 46 percent of the uses of the 230 chemicals—a substantial increase. Among the recommended restrictions are bans on a majority of uses of carbofuran, a product used for a variety of crops. EPA also announced its intention to ban major agricultural uses of the product lindane, a product targeted by environmental groups. Researchers at the University of California note problems with the elimination of so many products:

> Economic theory suggests that these increased restrictions and cancellations from the eventual implementation of the FQPA will result in reduced supply of commodities currently relying on [organophosphate] pesticides for pest control. This will result in higher prices for consumers and lower quantity [of produce] sold. . . . If consumers respond to the increased prices by reducing consumption of the affected fruits and vegetables (and perhaps consuming less

nutritious foods), they may suffer a loss of health benefits association with the change in consumption.(25)

Indeed, the researchers note that another study assessing the impacts of such laws reveals a potential negative health effect resulting from the FPQA.

Endnotes

(1) According to one National Research Council report, "The great majority of individual naturally occurring and synthetic chemicals in the diet appear to be present at levels below which any significant adverse biological effect is likely, and so low that they are unlikely to pose any appreciable cancer risk." See Committee on Comparative Toxicity of Naturally Occurring Carcinogens, Board on Environmental Studies and Toxicology, Commission on Life Sciences, National Research Council, *Carcinogens and Anticarcinogens in the Human Diet* (Washington, DC: National Academies Press, 1996), 336–37.

(2) The NRC is an affiliate of the National Academy of Sciences.

(3) Board on Agriculture, National Research Council, *Regulating Pesticides in Food: The Delaney Paradox* (Washington, DC: National Academies Press, 1987).

(4) Les v. Reilly, 968 F.2nd 985 (9th Cir. 1992), cert. denied, 113 U.S. 1361 (1993).

(5) See Joshua Lederberg, Robert E. Shope, and Stanley C. Oaks Jr., eds., *Emerging Infections: Microbial Threats to Health in the United States* (Washington, DC: National Academies Press, 1992), especially 163–67,

(6) Committee on Pesticides in the Diets of Infants and Children, National Research Council, *Pesticides in the Diets of Infants and Children* (Washington, DC: National Academies Press, 1993).

(7) Ibid., 359.

(8) 21 USC § 346a(b)(2)(A)(ii).

(9) After passage of the FQPA, Competitive Enterprise Institute's Jonathan Tolman noted in the *Wall Street Journal* that the 1996 law was more stringent than the old law and would lead to bans. A response by the Natural Resources Defense Council's Albert Meyerhoff concurred that the law was more stringent and would enable environmental groups to pursue bans. See Jonathan Tolman, "The Real Pests Aren't in the Food," *Wall Street Journal*, September 18, 1996, A18, and Albert H. Meyerhoff, "Law Makes Food Safer for Children," Letters to the Editor, *Wall Street Journal*, October 7, 1996, A23.

(10) 21 USC § 346a.

(11) For more information on endocrine disrupters, see "Endocrine Disrupters."

(12) See Draft User's Guide for the Endocrine Disrupter Priority Setting Database (Washington, DC: EPA and Eastern Research Group, 2000). A contractor produced this publication for the EPA. Page 1-1 states that the program will eventually help EPA "determine how best to regulate" chemicals.

(13) 21 USC § 346a(b)(2)(A)(ii).

(14) For an analysis, see Frank Cross, "The Consequences of Consensus: Dangerous Compromises of the Food Quality Protection Act," *Washington University Law Quarterly* 75, no. 3 (1997): 1155–206.

(15) The original study was Steven F. Arnold et al., "Synergistic Activation of Estrogen Receptor with Combinations of Environmental Chemicals," *Science* 272, no. 5267 (1996): 1489–92; the retraction is John A. McLachlan, "Synergistic

Effect of Environmental Estrogens: Report Withdrawn," *Science* 277, no. 5325 (1997): 459–463.

(16) Cross, "The Consequences of Consensus," 1174.

(17) Ibid., 1177.

(18) Sandra O. Archibald and Carl S. Winter, "Pesticides in Our Food," in *Chemicals in the Human Food Chain*, ed. Carl K. Winter, James N. Seiber, and Carole Nuckton (New York: Van Nostrand Reinhold, 1990), 39.

(19) Floyd J. Malveauz and Sheryl A. Fletcher-Vincent, "Environmental Factors of Childhood Asthma in Urban Centers," *Environmental Health Perspectives* 103, Suppl. 6 (1995): 59. See also the policy brief titled "Pesticides and Public Health."

(20) USDA, "EPA and Pesticide Registration Issues," Agricultural Research Service, Washington, DC, http://www.ars.usda.gov/is/np/mba/jan97/epa.htm.

(21) Glenn Hess, "EPA Phases out Pesticide Diazinon: Syngenta Cites Declining Margins." Chemical Market Reporter, December 11, 2000.

(22) Robert I. Rose, "Pesticides and Public Health: Integrated Methods of Mosquito Management," *Emerging Infectious Diseases* 7, no. 1 (January–February 2001): 17–23; http://www.cdc.gov/ncidod/eid/vol7no1/rose.htm.

(23)12. Sean B. Cash and Aaron Swoboda, "Food Quality Protection Act and California Agriculture," *Agricultural and Research Economics* Update 6, no. 4 (2003): 9–11, http://www.agecon.ucdavis.edu/extension/update/articles/v6n4_3.pdf.

(24) Kate Phillips, EPA Recommends Restrictions on Pesticide Usage, *Chemical Week* 168 no. 2 (August 9, 2006).

(25) Ibid., 10.

Organizations to Contact

The editors have compiled the following list of organizations concerned with the issues debated in this book. The descriptions are derived from materials provided by the organizations. All have publications or information available for interested readers. The list was compiled on the date of publication of the present volume; names, addresses, phone and fax numbers, and e-mail and Internet addresses may change. Be aware that many organizations take several weeks or longer to respond to inquiries, so allow as much time as possible.

CropLife America
1156 15th St. NW, Washington, DC   20005
(202) 296-1585
website: www.croplifeamerica.org

CropLife America is a nonadvocacy research and education nonprofit created in 2001 to promote and advance sustainable agriculture and the environmentally sound use of crop protection products (such as pesticides) and bioengineered agriculture. The organization's research focuses on the use of crop protection products within the agriculture industry and why these products are used, offering the first quantitative look at the benefits of crop protection products. CropLife America has produced presentations, articles, and written three comprehensive reports detailing these benefits. These major reports are entitled "The Value of Fungicides in U.S. Crop Production," "The Value of Herbicides in U.S. Crop Production," and "The Value of Insecticides in U.S. Crop Production." In 2006 the organization launched on its website the National Pesticide Use Database, the only national, comprehensive, publicly available pesticide use database.

GRACE Communications Foundation
215 Lexington Ave., New York, NY   10016
(212) 726-9161
website: www.gracelinks.org

GRACE Communications Foundation works to increase public awareness of the relationships among food, water, and energy systems in order to educate consumers and advocate for policies that address the environmental and public health effects of industrial food systems, support the development of sustainable food, conserve water resources, and provide clean energy alternatives. The Foundation has a food program, a water program, and an energy program, all aimed at advocating for more sustainable agriculture methods. For example, its food program and website—called Sustainable Table—provides information about the problems associated with industrial/high-pesticide agriculture and promotes sustainable farming and food consumption. The Foundation also publishes an online monthly newsletter called *GRACE Notes* and periodic brief updates on food, water, and energy issues called *GRACE Brief.*

National Pesticide Information Center (NPIC)
Oregon State University, 333 Weniger Hall
Corvallis, OR 97331-6502
(800) 858-7378
e-mail: npic@ace.orst.edu
website: http://npic.orst.edu

The National Pesticide Information Center (NPIC) provides objective, science-based information about pesticides and pesticide-related topics to enable people to make informed decisions about pesticides and their use. NPIC is a cooperative effort between Oregon State University and the US Environmental Protection Agency. NPIC serves as a source of factual, reliable information on pesticide chemistry, toxicology, environmental fate, regulations, and health effects. In addition, NPIC provides expert consultation to the medical community on human or animal pesticide exposure incidents, collects information on these incidents, and encourages reporting of these matters through a toll-free telephone line and other informational technology (IT) tools. The NPIC website contains sections on health and safety and the environment, as well as other topics related to pesticide use.

Natural Resources Defense Council (NRDC)
40 West 20th St., New York, NY   10011
(212) 727-2700 • fax: (212) 727-1773
website: www.nrdc.org

The Natural Resources Defense Council (NRDC) is a well-known environmental action group with over 1.3 million members and online activists and access to the expertise of hundreds of lawyers, scientists, and other professionals. The group works with businesses, elected leaders, and community groups on various environmental issues, including global warming, clean energy, reviving the world's oceans, defending endangered wildlife and wild places, preventing and cleaning up pollution, ensuring safe water, and fostering sustainable communities. The problem of pesticide pollution is an area targeted by the NRDC and a search of the group's website produces a long list of briefs, articles, and blogs on the topic. Examples include "Pesticides: What You Need to Know," "Minimizing Pesticides and Fertilizers," and "US Pesticide Trends—What, Where, and How Much."

Toxics Action Center
Eastern Massachusetts Office, 44 Winter St., 4th Floor
Boston, MA   02108
(617) 292-4821 • fax: (617) 292-8057
website: www.toxicsaction.org

The Toxics Action Center is a nonprofit that organizes communities throughout New England states to advocate for clean air and clean water and prevent or clean up pollution. Pesticide abuse is one of the pollution problems targeted by the Center and its website contains information about this issue as well as information to help citizens organize to take action to address this and other problems.

US Environmental Protection Agency (EPA), Office
of Pesticide Programs
1200 Pennsylvania Ave. NW, Washington, DC   20460

(703) 305-7090
website: www.epa.gov/pesticides

The US Environmental Protection Agency (EPA) is the main federal agency charged with protecting health and the environment. The EPA's Office of Pesticide Programs evaluates pesticides and other chemicals to safeguard people, threatened species, and ecosystems from environmental harm. Also, under the Federal Insecticide, Fungicide, and Rodenticide Act (FIFRA), the EPA and the states register or license pesticides for use in the United States, and anyone planning to import pesticides for use in the country must notify EPA. The agency's Office of Pesticide Programs website provides a wealth of information about pesticides, health and safety issues, environmental effects, controlling pests, pesticide regulation and enforcement, and other relevant topics. The website also contains a "Resources" section which lists various other federal agencies and nongovernmental organizations that deal with pesticide-related issues, as well as a list of databases and publications on the pesticide topic.

US Fish and Wildlife Service, Division
of Environmental Quality
4401 North Fairfax Dr., Suite 820, Arlington, VA   22203
(703) 358-2148
e-mail: EnvironmentalQuality@fws.gov
website: www.fws.gov

The US Fish and Wildlife Service is the main federal agency charged with protecting wildlife and their habitat from pollution of all types, including pesticides. The agency works to control pollution at the source from waste treatment facilities, mining, agriculture, and other sites in order to prevent or minimize contamination of fish, wildlife, and plants. In addition, the agency conducts field studies to investigate pollution effects and fish and wildlife die-offs from pesticides and other types of pollution. Finally, the service collects data that can be used to acquire compensation for resources lost or degraded by pollution, working with other federal agencies. One of the topics featured on the agency's website is "Pesticides and Wildlife" and that topic contains information about pesticide use as well as links to studies, literature, and other federal agencies that deal with the issue.

Bibliography

Books

Fern Marshall Bradley, Barbara W. Ellis, and Deborah L. Martin
The Organic Gardener's Handbook of Natural Pest and Disease Control: A Complete Guide to Maintaining a Healthy Garden and Yard the Earth-Friendly Way. Emmaus, PA: Rodale Books, 2010.

Claudia F. Brownlie
Eco-Friendly Dusts & Baits to Rid Your Home of Pests. Dallas, NC: Amithi Marketing, 2012.

Rachel Carson
Silent Spring. Boston, MA: Houghton Mifflin Company, 2002.

Jon Entine and The American Council on Science & Health
Scared to Death: How Chemophobia Threatens Public Health. New York: American Council on Science & Health, 2011.

Allan S. Felsot and The American Council on Science & Health
Pesticides and Health: Myths vs. Realities. New York: American Council on Science & Health, 2011.

W.H. Hallenbeck and K.M. Cunningham-Burns
Pesticides and Human Health. New York: Springer, 2011.

Jill Lindsey Harrison
Pesticide Drift and the Pursuit of Environmental Justice. Cambridge, MA: The MIT Press, 2011.

Frederick Kaufman — *Bet the Farm: How Food Stopped Being Food.* Hoboken, NJ: Wiley, 2012.

David Kinkela — *DDT and the American Century: Global Health, Environmental Politics, and the Pesticide That Changed the World.* Chapel Hill: The University of North Carolina Press, 2011.

William Kucewicz and The American Council on Science & Health — *Pesticides in Perspective.* New York: American Council on Science & Health, 2011.

Eric Lichtfouse — *Farming for Food and Water Security.* New York: Springer, 2012.

Robyn O'Brien and Rachel Kranz — *The Unhealthy Truth: One Mother's Shocking Investigation into the Dangers of America's Food Supply—and What Every Family Can Do to Protect Itself.* New York: Three Rivers Press, 2010.

Hamir S. Rathore and Leo M.L. Nollet — *Pesticides: Evaluation of Environmental Pollution.* Boca Raton, FL: CRC Press, 2012.

Marie-Monique Robin — *The World According to Monsanto.* New York: New Press, 2012.

Maria Rodale — *Organic Manifesto: How Organic Food Can Heal Our Planet, Feed the World, and Keep Us Safe.* Emmaus, PA: Rodale Books, 2011.

Thomas G. Spiro, Kathleen L. Purvis-Roberts, and William M. Stigliani — *Chemistry of the Environment.* Sausalito, CA: University Science Books, 2011.

Sandra Steingraber — *Living Downstream: An Ecologist's Personal Investigation of Cancer and the Environment.* Cambridge, MA: Da Capo Press, 2010.

Periodicals and Internet Sources

Mark Bittman — "Pesticides: Now More than Ever," *New York Times*, December 11, 2012. http://opinionator.blogs.nytimes.com.

Damian Carrington — "Pesticides Linked to Honeybee Decline," *The Guardian*, March 29, 2012. www.guardian.co.uk.

Aimin Chen and Wendy Hessler — "Chemical Exposures Cause Child IQ Losses That Rival Major Diseases," *Environmental Health News*, February 24, 2012. www.environmentalhealth news.org.

Caroline Cox — "No Guarantee of Safety," *Journal of Pesticide Reform*, vol. 17, no. 2, Summer 1997. www.pesticide.org.

David Suzuki Foundation — "Pesticides Bans Are Healthy for Environment and People," December 8, 2011. www.davidsuzuki.org/blogs.

John Entine	"Scientists, Journalists Challenge Claim That GM Crops Harm the Environment," *Forbes*, October 12, 2012. www.forbes.com.
Fox News	"What Are the Pros and Cons of Garden Pesticides?," April 12, 2012. www.foxnews.com.
Friends of the Earth	"50 Years After *Silent Spring*, 'Pesticides Still Pose Wildlife Threat,'" One World, September 27, 2012. http://oneworld.org.
Josie Garthwaite	"Superweeds, Superpests: The Legacy of Pesticides," *New York Times*, October 5, 2012. http://green.blogs.nytimes.com.
Ronnie Greene	"Poisoning Workers at the Bottom of the Food Chain," *Mother Jones*, June 25, 2012. www.motherjones.com.
Beth Hoffman	"Are Pesticides Safe? It Depends Who You Trust," *Forbes*, June 20, 2012. www.forbes.com.
Beth Hoffman	"Five Reasons to Eat Organic Apples: Pesticides, Healthy Communities, and You," *Forbes*, April 23, 2012. www.forbes.com.
Brett Israel	"Widely Used Pesticide Seems to Harm Boys' Brains More than Girls," *Environmental Health News*, August 20, 2012. www.environmentalhealthnews.org.

Lindsey Konkel "Women at Risk: Health Problems Linked to Environmental Estrogens," *Environmental Health News*, July 31, 2012. www.environmentalhealth news.org.

Maureen Langlois "Organic Pesticides Not an Oxymoron," National Public Radio, June 17, 2011. www.npr.org/blogs.

Edithe M. Lederer "U.N.: Chemicals Damaging Health and Environment," *USA Today*, September 6, 2012. www.usatoday .com.

LexisNexis Litigation Resource Community Staff "The Cost of Environmental Damage: Refineries, Pesticide Manufacturer Pay Out $150 Million in Recent Settlements of Separate Suits," *LexisNexis*, June 19, 2012. www.lexisnexis.com.

Timothy Martinez Jr. "Legal Bird Pesticide to Blame for Dozens of Dead Birds in NJ," *Into the Air*, August 20, 2012. www .backyardchirper.com/blog.

Anne C. Mulkern "Pesticide Industry Ramps Up Lobbying in Bid to Pare EPA Rules," *New York Times*, February 24, 2011. www.nytimes.com.

Alison Rourke "Great Barrier Reef Suffering from Australia's Decision to Allow Pesticides," *The Guardian*, March 27, 2012. www.guardian.co.uk.

Alexandra   "Study Links Food Allergies to
Sifferlin   Pesticides in Tap Water," *TIME*,
                 December 3, 2012. http://healthland
                 .time.com.

Christie Wilcox "Mythbusting 101: Organic Farming
                 > Conventional Agriculture,"
                 Scientific American, July 18, 2011.
                 http://blogs.scientificamerican.com.

Index

D

E